HACKING
LEADERSHIP

HACKING LEADERSHIP

10 Ways Great Leaders Create Schools That Teachers, Students, and Parents Love

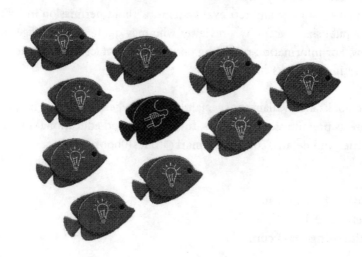

Joe Sanfelippo
Tony Sinanis

PUBLICATIONS

Hacking Leadership
© 2016 by Times 10 Publications

These books are available at special discounts when purchased in quantity for use as premiums, promotions, fundraising, and educational use. For inquiries and details, contact us: mark@times10books.com

Published by Times 10
Cleveland, OH
hacklearningseries.com

Cover Design by Tracey Henterly
Interior Design by Steven Plummer
Editing by Ruth Arseneault
Proofreading by Jennifer Jas

Library of Congress Control Number: 2016934739
ISBN: 978-0-9861049-4-7
First Printing: June, 2016

CONTENTS

ACKNOWLEDGEMENTS

W E WOULD BOTH like to acknowledge that this book could not happen without the opportunity to lead given to us by the Fall Creek School District and Cantiague Elementary. To the staff, families, and kids…thank you. You are the reason we do what we do and a simple "thanks" does not even begin to express our gratitude. We would also like to thank all the educators (teachers, coaches, principals, superintendents, and everyone else) in our Personal Learning Network (PLN). They have pushed our thinking, expanded our perspectives, and helped us enhance our craft. Their willingness to share ideas, passions, and beliefs has been a source of inspiration for us and our work.

Joe: I would like to thank Andrea for the unwavering support through the long evenings and stress that comes with leadership. To the three crazy kids who call me dad: You are amazing and make me proud every second of every day. You are all going to be incredible leaders.

Tony: Thanks to Paul for inspiring me to be the best dad, educator, and person possible. Your strength, courage, and positivity sustain me and bring more joy than I thought possible. I love you, kid! To Feli, thank you for making my dreams come true and for loving me unconditionally—it is an honor to share my world with you! And to my family, thank you for supporting me and always making me smile!

PUBLISHER'S FOREWORD

WOULD YOU WANT to work for you? Would you enjoy being a teacher or a student at your school? Do you enter the building with a smile on your face, anticipating a day of inspiration, excitement, and joy? Is there any hesitation in your answers? Be honest.

School district superintendent Joe Sanfelippo and building principal Tony Sinanis definitely answer yes to all of these questions. And they don't just tell me how much they love what they do; they proclaim it to the world on their social networks, blogs, and their popular *Successful Schools* podcast. Unfortunately, the authors of *Hacking Leadership* are more the exception than the rule when it comes to how leaders lead.

Please understand: This is not an indictment of individuals who lead. It is a statement about a system that often inhibits potentially great leaders. Most administrators, I assume, have good intentions. Unfortunately, many have become victims of a bureaucracy that makes effective leadership difficult. As policymakers and lobbyists continue their quests to standardize education, increase high stakes testing, and politicize learning, decision makers face challenges that didn't exist just twenty years ago. Today's education model promotes accountability through test scores and college and career readiness, at all costs—a system that pressures some leaders into decisions that they regret.

Fortunately, there is still hope for all of our leaders, teachers, parents and, most important, our children. Hope that education can be saved from bad policy and misguided policy-makers. Hope that we can successfully navigate standardization and testing. Hope that teaching and learning can be fun again. These hopes will become reality if every school leader heeds the advice contained in this book, written by two progressive-minded leaders who understand how to create a marvelous culture of learning that all stakeholders love—no matter what seemingly impenetrable dams may stand in their way.

Hacking Leadership is the fifth book in the *Hack Learning Series*. Our authors are all education hackers; that is, they strive to solve problems with right-now solutions that don't require the cliché five-year plan.

Education hackers are tinkerers and fixers. Like all hackers, they see solutions to problems that other people do not see. The label "hacker" originated in the field of technology, referring to those who circumvented or subverted systems to make innovations. Steve Jobs and Mark Zuckerberg might be considered technology's greatest hackers. No one taught them how to build an operating system or a social network, but they saw possibilities that others couldn't see.

Like Jobs and Zuckerberg, our hackers see things through a different lens. They are specialists who love to grapple with problems that need to be turned upside down and viewed from another perspective. The fix may appear unreasonable to those plagued by the issue, but to the hacker the solution is evident, and with a little hacking it will be as clear and elegant as a gracefully-designed smartphone or a powerful social network.

INSIDE THE BOOKS

Each book in the series contains chapters, called Hacks, which are composed of these sections:

- **The Problem:** Something educators are currently wrestling with that doesn't yet have a clear-cut solution.

- **The Hack:** A brief description of the author's unique solution.

- **What You Can Do Tomorrow:** Ways you can take the basic hack and implement it right away in bare-bones form.

- **Blueprint for Full Implementation:** A step-by-step system for building long-term capacity.

- **Overcoming Pushback:** A list of possible objections you might come up against in your attempt to implement this hack and how to overcome them.

- **The Hack in Action:** A snapshot of an educator or group of educators who have used this hack in their work and how they did it.

I am proud to be a contributing author and publisher of the *Hack Learning Series*, which is changing how we view and solve problems. When you finish reading this book, you will understand how to unravel the complexities of leadership. You may see solutions to other problems that you've previously overlooked. In the end, you might even become a hacker. And that's a good thing.

—MARK BARNES, AUTHOR, PUBLISHER, EDUCATION HACKER

INTRODUCTION
A better way

S PEND THIRTY MINUTES watching a leader interact with members of the school community and you will be able to determine her stance on leadership and discover whether she embraces the hacking leadership mindset. Education hackers challenge the status quo and see a problem as an opportunity to try various solutions. Hacking school leadership is about empowering other people so they can achieve their hopes, dreams, and goals. Whether working with students, teachers, or family members, a school leader's objective must be to remove barriers and help transform perceived problems into opportunities and possibilities.

The daily work of a school leader is no longer just being an administrator or manager or even a boss; instead, a school leader needs to model transformative practices so that innovating becomes a norm and working with common principles becomes a collective goal for community members. Sitting in an office checking emails and efficiently completing paperwork does not fulfill the needs of the modern school. Effective leaders put learning at the center of daily work. The time has come to hack traditional school practices to emphasize authentic and personalized learning experiences, not just policies, mandates, and test scores.

When school leaders embrace the opportunity to lead with heart, healthy relationships unfold within the community, inspiring practices that are in children's best interests. With a leader's impact and direction, these relationships underpin the culture of a school. All members of the community contribute to and perpetuate the culture of a building, but the school leader sets the tone and has the greatest single influence on a school's positive or negative culture.

Culture is predicated on and expressed in feelings and emotions, but there are still tangible signals that indicate a school's culture. The parking lot and exterior of the building give an initial impression—a poorly maintained exterior communicates a different attitude than a well-manicured and inviting exterior does. An even more accurate impression results from the way the main office team greets a visitor. You can get a pretty good read on the school's climate based on whether you're offered a warm smile and welcome or have no one look up to acknowledge your presence.

Spending thirty minutes with the principal puts a human face on the culture and helps solidify your understanding of it. Does the principal communicate positive, healthy, and compassionate relationships with all members of the community or stay in the office and complain about the staff? A principal's demeanor and attitude clearly indicate the culture and signal what could be happening throughout the school.

We believe that schools can offer inspiration, hope, and opportunity to both children and adults. Leadership determines if a school has a significant purpose and whether it meets that purpose effectively. Educators who are ready to hack school leadership want children to feel loved, safe, and empowered as learners and as individuals.

Leaders who employ a hacker's mindset want kids to discover things they didn't even realize existed or were possible. They want teachers and family members to know that they matter and that they have a voice in what happens in their school. Hacking school leadership means considering what schools could be tomorrow and making that a reality today.

Cultivating a forward-thinking environment involves setting the stage for the amazing to happen and giving all members of the community space to be the best they can be. Too often students, educators, and families experience multiple new initiatives at once, each implemented in the hope that it will be the magic potion that fixes the many problems that afflict the school district. We know that the Band-Aid solutions offered by many initiatives or standardized curriculum do not affect sustainable improvement and change.

> **Because a school's culture extends to all of its stakeholders, effective interactions are the single most important non-negotiable in creating flourishing schools.**

If we want to move past trendy, superficial solutions, we must begin by hacking leadership. Preparing the environment through an innovative leadership approach is essential for long-term success. We believe our schools should be playgrounds of creativity, not places where content is merely memorized and repeated.

If leaders allow staff creative influence and establish an environment that values creativity, learners win. Effective communication is critical to moving a school from having isolated moments of excellence to working consistently at a superior level. In excellent schools, all participants feel valued and contribute to the positive narrative.

Successful school cultures facilitate communication between teams, between leadership and staff, between school and community. Because a school's culture extends to all of its stakeholders, effective interactions are the single most important non-negotiable in creating flourishing schools. And these schools and their leaders aren't born; they have to be hacked.

HACK 1

BE PRESENT AND ENGAGED

Lead learners are visible

*Example is not the main thing in influencing
others, it is the only thing.*
—ALBERT SCHWEITZER, THEOLOGIAN AND PHILOSOPHER

THE PROBLEM: SCHOOLS ARE RUN BY
MANAGERS, NOT LEADERS

WHEN WE ASKED educators to list the words they associate with school principals, their responses included: boss, disciplinarian, supervisor, decision-maker, manager, evaluator, disconnected, and isolated. Although all these words are not necessarily negative, they don't paint the most positive picture of school leaders. None of these labels speak to the notion of being an instructional leader or a visionary, or to accessing 21st century skills to engage in learning. They describe a more traditional principal, a manager who oversees the organization and handles the problems from a comfortable chair in the office. Perceptions of a principal's job have not evolved very much from those of the early 20th century, when the principal was expected to manage the school from the office while having very little to do with the children, the teachers, the learning, or the instruction.

While acting as manager, disciplinarian, and evaluator are all real and important aspects of a principal's job, they are not the only tasks necessary to lead a school successfully. Unfortunately, many principals still focus primarily on those traditional aspects of their work. These old-school leaders deal with administrative tasks, rarely interacting with members of the community. Learning is not their priority, so they spend little time engaging with children and teachers or being present in classrooms. They choose not to invest in developing the "soft skills" necessary to nurture healthy relationships with all members of the community. They don't understand a leader's direct impact on school culture or recognize that every decision they make affects that culture's trajectory. Because these administrators see themselves as bosses, they miss opportunities to be effective leaders who bring about positive and sustainable change.

THE HACK: BE PRESENT AND ENGAGED

Administrators who focus primarily on being the boss are not present enough to be truly effective. Today's students, teachers, and families require more from their principals. Communities need school leaders who understand the direct impact leadership has on school culture. They want leaders who prioritize learning and who lead with heart. Today's administrators must learn to invest in nurturing healthy, positive relationships that are rooted in trust and respect. Healthy relationships are at the core of any highly successful school or district.

What better way to be engaged with the learning in your school than by actually facilitating the learning?

Although there are dozens of places to start building relationships in a school community, our primary focus should always be the children, so start there. Kids intuitively connect with people they trust and respect; make yourself available and earn that trust.

Smile. Be transparent. Listen. Lead with joy. When we have confidence that relationships are as important to educational philosophy as differentiation, standards, and instructional techniques, we can take connections with our students to a higher level. Relationships rooted in trust, respect, and compassion can take a nice school and make it an extraordinary space where excitement and passion become palpable. When our kids know that we value them personally, they will develop higher levels of self-confidence and feel safe enough in their environment to take risks with their learning.

Most educators will readily agree that relationships can have a positive impact on the kids, but it doesn't end there. We must also develop relationships with adults: Teachers, custodians, secretaries, families, teacher aides, bus drivers, and all other members of the school community need to feel confident in shared trust and respect.

Foster trust by being collaborative. Decisions should rarely be made in isolation; instead, all members of the school community should have some voice, and it is your responsibility to listen to others—to be present—in order to broaden your perspective and make the best decisions possible.

To make genuine leadership the new norm in our schools, school leaders need to invest in relationships. They must be visible and involved in the classroom, the lunchroom, and the bus line. Today's leaders must move away from the title of administrator and become lead learners who are guided by doing what is in the best interest of children.

WHAT YOU CAN DO TOMORROW

The prospect of becoming an engaged and present school leader can be daunting because there is only one of you and hundreds of everyone else. This reality is not changing, so start small. Make one consistent change at a time until it becomes a habit in your practice.

- **Just listen.** Reserve at least two 15-minute blocks on your calendar each day for relationship building. During that time, check in with two different members of the community to find out how things are going. Open your ears to kids, teachers, parents, secretaries, colleagues, supervisors, and don't just *listen* to them—you have to actually *hear* them. Hear what they say, hear what they feel, hear what they need, hear what they perceive. Pay attention to every word, because they will share critical information that will strengthen your relationship. Keep a list of the people you have spoken with so you can make sure that everyone is heard.

- **Ask questions.** Find out how things are going in general by sending a question to staff, students, or families. You can do this via a Google Form, a Twitter poll, a query to a Voxer group, or an email. Your question might be geared toward anything from getting a sense of staff morale to learning about community concerns. Follow up on the information you glean from the responses. We may not be able to connect on a face-to-face level with all members of the community each day but we can still allow them to be heard using digital platforms.

- **Make time for lunch with kids.** Informal, but planned, exchanges with students can provide critical insight that is not available from any other source. At Cantiague Tony regularly makes time to have lunch with kids. Sometimes they ask for a lunch date; sometimes they earn it as a reward for something they have done in the classroom; at other times Tony has a free block of time and he pulls a group of kids aside for some lunch and chatting. Although not all children feel comfortable having lunch with their principal, inviting students in a group (six or fewer is ideal) will give them enough social support to loosen them up quickly and they will chat it up the entire lunch period. Even though it's great to talk about everything from weekend plans to the group's favorite songs, make sure to be intentional about some of the questions asked during the lunch "meeting" to elicit information from the children about how school is going from their perspective. Ask them what they love about the school day; ask them about their favorite times of the week; ask them about the experiences they could do without; and ask them how we could make school better for them. Remember, schools should be more about the kids and less about the adults.

- **Celebrate in public.** Construct a real-time narrative that shows the community how dynamic and relevant school can be. You can easily accomplish this right away by creating a social media account for your school. It might be Twitter, Instagram, Snapchat, or any other medium that you already feel comfortable with. Make a post a day to share something amazing that is happening in your space. This one account will initiate a re-branding of your school, allowing you to create an identity by telling your story. Your school's positive social media presence will help to counteract negative impressions that your community might have about school. Even though the media typically bashes public education and the landscape of education is not always a pretty one, we can have a voice in the discourse. Publicizing daily celebrations can be your entry point.

- **Get out of your office.** Open your calendar and block out time in the day to be visible, engaged, and present. Altogether, aim to spend about an hour's worth of time outside your office. Transformative leaders don't change the world by sending emails or scheduling meetings: Get out and engage with students, teachers, and anyone else you encounter. Ask teachers how to support their efforts. Spend time in the classrooms asking children what they are learning and why it is important—these two questions will give you insight into class dynamics and allow you to collect data you can use to plan for future PD. Play with kids during recess or lunch so they understand they are important to you and that you are always available to them. The informal conversations that will unfold during these times can be incredibly telling. You'll get a real perspective on how school looks or feels to kids. You must get out of the office if you are going to make the shift from administrator to leader.

A BLUEPRINT FOR FULL IMPLEMENTATION

Step 1: Start every school day with personal interactions.

Tony arrives at school at least one hour before the day officially begins so he can connect with people before the day gets hectic. He uses this time to chat informally with his main office team, the custodial crew, classroom teachers, teacher aides, and anyone else who might be in the building. For the purposes of efficiency and equity, Tony keeps a staff list on the corner of his desk so he can cross off people he speaks to each morning to make sure he connects with everyone at least once each month. Tony intentionally chooses to have these chats in the morning when most people are in a positive state of mind, ready to go, and not exhausted from the day. Once students begin to arrive, Tony heads outside to make morning connections with the kids, striving to greet as many as possible by name—knowing kids' names makes a difference.

Step 2: Use morning announcements to kick start community.

Establish community every morning as you share important information and relevant updates over the loudspeaker. Use this morning routine to engage all members from the moment they walk in and to remind everyone that your school is a close community. Students will enjoy opportunities to lead the pledge, read the announcements, or advertise school events. Although Cantiague students hear some standard announcements each day, the children may also get to include other appropriate announcements, such as a joke, facts about the date in history, or other important school-wide information.

Put a system in place to include kids in this process instead of choosing students at random. For example, Cantiague children know that the main office has blank calendars available so they can sign up to do the morning announcements up to two months in advance. Letting students sign up empowers them to be responsible, allows them to control the timeframe and have a say in the content, and gives them a voice in the school community.

As the leader of the building, make sure you are part of the morning in a special way. Tony announces student and staff birthdays each day, allowing the whole community to participate in birthday celebrations. We cap off the birthday announcements with a birthday selfie that is posted on all our social media platforms. (Thank you to Minnesota principal Brad Gustafson for that idea.)

Step 3: Cover classes to give teachers planning time.

What better way to be engaged with the learning in your school than by actually facilitating the learning? Whether you do an activity with kids to relieve a group of teachers so they can plan, or cover a class for the whole day when you are short of substitutes, spend uninterrupted time in classrooms. This allows you to connect with kids and shows that you value your teachers. They'll be delighted that you understand their need for planning time.

Step 4: Start a voluntary club during recess.

After years of hearing about how much kids love Minecraft and then watching some of our teachers use it meaningfully during various lessons, I decided I wanted to learn more about the game, so I started a voluntary Minecraft recess club at Cantiague. One day a week the library is open for kids to come and play Minecraft using the library's iPads or their own devices. This has been an amazing opportunity for me to hear kids talk about a topic they are passionate about and cannot wait to share. Your club doesn't have to be about Minecraft, it can be a writing club or a drawing club or a reading club. The point is you create a designated time and space to engage with kids on their terms.

Step 5: Blog to be transparent and reflective.

Start a blog to share your educational philosophies and beliefs so the community understands your position about various mandates, policies, or trends in education. This is another way for the community to engage with leadership, as blogs can often begin a conversation in the comments section. Another important byproduct of blogging is the opportunity to reflect, which provides positive professional development for educators—we can see where we have been and plan where we want to go.

Step 6: Create a "dream team."

A school leader spends much of his or her time reacting to situations and trying to solve problems. While that will always be true, it's more efficient to be proactive. In the short term, consider all possible consequences when making decisions. Then look to the future by engaging in discussions to define the ideal school and think about how to make that ideal a reality for your community. Start small and create a voluntary team made up of staff, families, and students to generate ideas about how the school can continue to move forward. Call it the "dream team" and work together to transform your school. Defining the ideal school together is a great strategy for being present because it allows a leader to engage in face-to-face conversations about things that matter to all constituent groups.

OVERCOMING PUSHBACK

Although being a visible, engaged, and present school lead learner is clearly a worthy goal, the reality is that many people meet change with resistance. Some teachers may not be comfortable with their principal or superintendent visiting their classrooms on a regular basis. Some children may not want to include the principal in their basketball game at recess because that is just weird. Some parents may not be used to having contact with the principal for any reason except a problem. Any effort to hack school administration will lead to some amount of pushback.

Teachers don't like when I am in their classrooms. Traditionally, a school leader only shows up in someone's classroom to conduct a formal observation or to discuss some sort of problem, which of course perpetuates the "us versus them" mentality. In this model, when a school leader walks into a classroom the teacher gets stressed and questions the motivation for the visit. In fact, for many teachers, administrative visits feel like contrived "gotcha" moments where the leader is trying to catch them doing something wrong.

The fault in that perception lies not with the teacher but with the school leader. When a leader spends more time in the office or out of the building in meetings than in classrooms, then his or her sudden presence at the classroom door will certainly be received as questionable at best. The only way to change this situation is by dropping in on every classroom every day and engaging appropriately while there. Check your judgment at the door and be open to learning.

Granted, in larger schools it may not be feasible for the principal to get into every classroom every day. That is when other building leaders such as assistant principals and department chairs become part of the process. Divide the school up between the leaders so every classroom gets a visit each day and rotate the assignments so the principal gets to see every classroom at least once a week.

What does a visit to the classroom look like? That is up to you, but treat the opportunity as an important one. Talk to kids and to teachers; engage in the lesson, if that seems appropriate; sit quietly and watch from the back without necessarily taking notes; take pictures of what is happening and share them on social media. Whatever you do, be engaged and make your presence as non-threatening as possible. Understand that these daily visits to classrooms are opportunities to build relationships, to understand how learning unfolds in your school, to inform your practice so you can support the community effectively.

Things have changed since I was in the classroom, so teachers might question my feedback. Many teachers feel skeptical of school leaders who have left the classroom and gone over to the "dark side" of education. For these teachers, school administration seems disconnected from the classroom, disengaged from kids, and detached from teachers. The commonplace wisdom is that educational leaders don't understand the daily pressures and expectati classrooms because they have left the trenches and no lc firsthand experience.

Combating this disconnect is enough reason for school leaders to be in classrooms every single day. If we are going to understand what teaching and learning feel like in a school, we must engage in it on some level by being present in the classrooms. If we are going to understand what resources will enhance instruction, we need to be engaged in the learning and teaching. If we are going to help reframe problems, we must identify and engage with those problems. When we acknowledge that the classroom may have changed since we last taught, it makes sense to make being in the classroom a priority and not an afterthought.

People expect a timely response to emails. Colleagues and supervisors may object to the time lapse in your responses if you spend the majority of your workday outside your office, as both of us do. Although such a leader may be called unresponsive, the truth is that choosing to participate fully in the life of the school often means leaving most of the administrative work, including checking emails, until after school. While we understand that some people use email to communicate urgent matters and look for an immediate response, we spend our time in the classrooms, lunchroom, and hallways, because that is where our kids and teachers are and that is where we need to be as leaders.

Fortunately, our staff members and colleagues have come to understand that we are rarely in our offices because we put the kids first. With that being said, sometimes a leader needs to attend to administrative matters that will have a direct impact on instruction. Our solution is to include our work email on our phones so that we can check it throughout the day and respond quickly to anything that requires immediate attention. We have also given our cell phone numbers to colleagues because their time is valuable and we want them to be able to reach us if something urgent happens. All non-essential messages wait until we have made our rounds in the building. Colleagues and supervisors will eventually understand that being visible, present, and engaged is a necessary step in becoming a transformational instructional lead learner.

THE HACK IN ACTION

When you shift from being administrator to instructional lead learner you realize it is all about you and not at all about you at the same time. The position of school leader is a critical one that affects every person in the educational community. The leader shapes the culture, tone, and climate of the entire community. To that end, the community expects capable lead learners, transformational educators who are knowledgeable about current and sustainable instructional techniques.

Tony's Story

A couple of years ago Joe Mazza tweeted that he uses the term "lead learner" to describe his work as an elementary principal. I started researching this term and repeatedly came across statements from thinkers like Fullan and Marzano, which stressed how important it is for a principal to be an instructional leader who focuses specifically on the learning of the staff, the students, and the community. The more I read, the more I realized that as a principal I devote the majority of my time and energy to the learning of those around me. I am passionate about learning, teaching, curriculum, and instruction, so these aspects of my work naturally feel significant to me. I realized I am a lead learner—one of many in our school community— because I model the importance of learning through my own daily actions and I support and facilitate the learning of those around me. Of course simply modeling the work of a lead learner is not enough. Administrators who are ready to hack leadership must encourage students, staff, and families to embrace opportunities to become lead learners. In highly effective schools or districts, everyone has a hand in leading the learning.

Among thousands of other actions, the lead learner who is ready to hack can be the one who:

- models learning,

- offers an open ear when someone is struggling,

- initiates a spirit day when it's been a long month and the students and staff need a little fun,

- advocates for the needs of the students and staff,

- removes obstacles so the staff can maximize their teaching by taking risks,

- meets with the parents who feel their child has been wronged,

- presents a sound case to a board member that an additional classroom section would be beneficial to children.

The school leader can do a *lot*, so on some level the focus is on you as the leader, but it is not on you as an individual. To that end, try not to take yourself too seriously. You've not reached a pinnacle that means you don't need to learn and grow anymore, so exhibit some humility and open a book. Sitting in your office all day and dictating to everyone around you will not set anyone up for success, nor will it endear people to you. Neither is it profitable to employ a fixed mindset or allow institutional biases to continue because of your personal position or thinking. Be a school leader who takes the work seriously and pours heart and soul into the school community, but at the same time keep your ego in check.

School leaders who are present and engaged understand that politics pervades education, so you must take the time to develop and nurture relationships. When you invest time in connecting with members of all constituent groups, you slowly amass social capital, and that social capital becomes your "Get Out of Jail" card when navigating a particularly political situation.

The truth is, most people in an educational community have an agenda (even the leader), and it is the school leader's responsibility to gain people's trust and to understand the various agendas so they can be aligned in the best interests of children and the community. Don't waste your energy on worrying about being liked—at some point, every member in the community will dislike you for one reason or another. Instead, expend energy on founding healthy relationships on trust and confidence. Remember, it is not about you but it can be about the politics, so healthy relationships must be at the core of the community.

Be intentional about every conversation and exchange. Educational leaders need to spend more time in discussion with staff than just chatting in passing or after an observation. Set aside "sacred" time to talk about learning, schedule meetings to discuss instructional practices, meet as teams to discuss students' readiness levels and what actions will best meet their needs. We need to make time to just talk about learning and teaching, about successes and failures. Just talk, but with focus and intentionality, because those conversations fill in the picture of what is going on in our buildings and help us best meet the needs of our learners.

Although hacking school leadership involves enacting many changes in our practices, the first and most important change transforms a principal from a disengaged administrator to an instructional lead learner who is visible, present, and engaged in every aspect of the school community. Yes, we still need to make the time to check emails, participate in meetings, and complete everything else on our "To Do" lists, but we can't be bound to our desks or offices. The kind of leader our schools need leads with the heart and mind, spending time building relationships instead of doing managerial tasks. Transformational lead learners understand the impact they have on school culture, and therefore they strive to build a culture that has a positive influence on the school's trajectory.

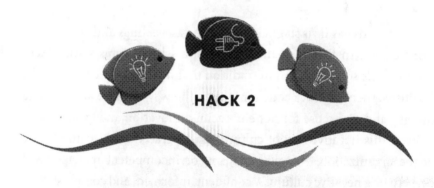

HACK 2

CREATE C.U.L.T.U.R.E.

Start with school leaders

If you get the culture right, most of the other stuff will just happen naturally on its own.
—TONY HSIEH, CEO, ZAPPOS.COM

THE PROBLEM: SCHOOL LEADERS
UNDERESTIMATE THEIR IMPACT

ALTHOUGH SCHOOL CULTURE can be defined and described in many ways, every definition ultimately circles back to leadership. A school leader doesn't single-handedly create the school's culture, but that one person does have the greatest impact on the way a school's culture feels. The actions of many—students, staff, families—express and perpetuate that culture, but the tone and leadership style of the school leader thrust the school into a positive or negative trajectory.

One of the tricky aspects of defining a school's culture is that it's not a fixed entity. Culture reflects the feelings and perceptions people experience in a school, which in a healthy environment evolve over time. Many variables cause school culture to transform itself, unless the school's dynamic is stagnant, in which case feelings and perceptions won't evolve. In that case, the culture of a school seems static, fixed. Culture feels so entrenched in tradition that no change seems possible. "Culture" then becomes code for "this is the way we have always done things," and an excuse for not embracing innovation and evolution.

Even this negative school culture can be traced back to the leader of the organization. A staid, arrogant, or incompetent manager will perpetuate a negative culture. A confident, informed, and compassionate instructional lead learner will propagate a positive culture. Creating a positive school culture is a responsibility any school leader must recognize and take seriously.

THE HACK: NURTURE A POSITIVE C.U.L.T.U.R.E.

Any successful hack of a school necessitates developing an understanding of that particular culture, determining how it feels to the educators within the organization. We created the acronym C.U.L.T.U.R.E. to help school leaders with this hack:

Communication
Uncovers
Learning
Transparency
Ultimately
Reveals
Everything

Communication is the beating heart of school culture. The positive impact of an accessible school leader who communicates well and relates well with others circulates throughout the entire system. Clear, consistent communication fosters transparency so all members of the school community share important information. Whether the communication is about curricular decisions that affect teachers or changes in policy that concern students and their families, if leaders communicate in a genuine way, the trust they earn contributes to an even more positive environment. Be aware, though, that constant communication and transparent practice have positive effects only if a school leader can personally validate that his or her decisions have been made to benefit the children.

When the culture values the important work of learners and educators, a school's focus centers exactly where it should. On the learning. School culture cannot be separated from school leaders, because the actions of the individual directly shape and influence the organization's norms.

After amplifying the school's culture and collective vision beyond the walls of your school, pause and ask those around you how that message is resonating with them.

As educator and author, Todd Whitaker, shared in his book *What Great Principals Do Differently*, if the principal sneezes the whole school community catches a cold. As leaders, whether of the school or the classroom, we set the tone for the space. What we value and emphasize eventually permeates the classroom or building. If we focus on mandates, policies, and test scores, then that will set the tone in the building; that will become the culture of the space. Since we have a tremendous impact on the culture, keep it positive and build healthy relationships with all members of the community to reinforce a positive and productive culture.

WHAT YOU CAN DO TOMORROW

The prospect of shaping a school's culture can be overwhelming for a leader because of its abstract nature. Unfortunately, thinking about it will not effect change; instead of being stifled by trepidation, a leader must take action. Since communication can have the greatest impact, that is the perfect place to start hacking school culture.

- **Feed people.** If you have inherited a school where the culture is hard to conceptualize or define, then make time for informal discussions and relationship-building. One of the best ways to facilitate these informal gatherings is to feed people, because being together around food helps people get comfortable; they will linger and information will flow more readily. Whether it means keeping a bowl of candy in your office, getting bagels for breakfast, or ordering pizza for lunch, feed teachers often. Conversation will grow and you will begin to find the pulse of the staff, which is the perfect starting point for building culture.

- **Define the status of your school's culture.** It is surprising how infrequently school leaders talk explicitly about school culture with members of the community. Although it's common to discuss collective vision, non-negotiable priorities, or educational philosophy, it's less usual to initiate dialogue on this significant dynamic. Defining and reflecting on the current status is the best first step to initiating effective change. You can gather information virtually through a survey or personally during a faculty gathering, but it is important that the conversation starts with the staff. Culture begins within the building and spreads beyond it. Pose the following questions to your staff in advance of discussing them in a face-to-face meeting:

  1. *What is the culture of our school?*

  2. *What makes our school different than any other school?*

3. What feelings and emotions are evoked when you think about our school?

4. How can we continue to shape the trajectory of the culture in positive ways?

- **Share the communication plan with families.** Once you have defined the school's culture with your team, decide how you will communicate it and all the other amazing things happening in your school with your families. Schools can no longer function as fortresses that close out the surrounding community; instead, creating high levels of transparency through a constant flow of communication is critical. Families should have access to relevant and dynamic information. We must harness the power of digital tools to help accelerate and amplify our story beyond the walls of our schools. Pick one platform—maybe Facebook or Twitter or Google Docs—and start sharing the different aspects of your school's C.U.L.T.U.R.E.

- **Name social media interns of the week.** Make visible the wonderful educational opportunities that educators are giving your students and let the kids relay that information. Embrace the possibilities of students telling their stories by implementing a "social media intern" or "tweeter of the week" program in your school. (You might create an "Instagrammer of the week" or "Snapchatter of the week" if Twitter is not your preferred platform.) Classroom teachers could assign students to take on this job for the week to tell their classroom's stories via the social media account. Before turning control over to the students, the teacher could put any necessary parameters in place. For example, "The teacher must approve any post before it goes live." In the primary grades, where the children may not be ready to navigate a social media platform, create the job of "photographer of the week" so the students can capture images that an adult will share on social media posts. Schools have incredible stories and children are some of the best storytellers, so empower them to shape the narrative of your school.

A BLUEPRINT FOR FULL IMPLEMENTATION

Step 1: Build ongoing communication with all stakeholders.

Once you have developed an understanding of school culture, share your findings. Disseminate the message, "This is who we are and this is where we are headed together," in emails, newsletters, video updates, and face-to-face encounters. Make sure that this message features the locations where stakeholders meet: PTA meetings, faculty gatherings, social media. Taking care to be consistent in the way the school gets presented develops a cohesive understanding throughout the community.

Step 2: Educate families and staff.

The reality is that some families have a negative perception about social media, so it is imperative that they are educated about any platforms you are using. For example, if you decide to start with Twitter, hold several Twitter 101 sessions at times that are convenient for both families and staff to attend. Make sure to publicize the sessions in advance so people can save the date. Provide people with information and resources via email and through handouts during the sessions to correct any skewed perceptions they may have about social media. Show them how it works, show them how it will be used, and give them time to set up an account and explore the platform themselves. Finally, consider having someone record your session so it can be shared with anyone who couldn't attend.

Step 3: Ask questions.

After amplifying the school's culture and collective vision beyond the walls of your school, pause and ask those around you how that message is resonating with them. Question members from a cross section of the community to take the "temperature" of how people are responding to the school story. Ask for feedback during informal conversations at the drop off/pick up areas, before or after PTA meetings, while you are passing through the faculty lounge, or via a short survey of no more than three questions that will take five minutes or less to answer. Although informal face-to-face conversations will perhaps give you more information because they allow you to register tone of voice, body language, and eye contact, the survey allows everyone to participate. If the message "sticks" on both personal and professional levels, then you have achieved sustainability. Even once you judge the culture to be sustainable, continue to ask questions, but don't limit it to only once a year—take a reading of the culture at least four or five times a year.

Step 4: Hand the microphone over to the community.

After it is clear that your school culture is in a positive state and everyone is aware of the common vision, empower all members of the community to share the school's stories from their perspectives. For example, every week at Cantiague Elementary, six students from each class research what's happening at each grade level and film their updates to share from the school YouTube channel. Showing what's happening in your school supports and inspires the staff, validates and encourages the students, and informs and enlightens the broader community about the school's C.U.L.T.U.R.E. We make the video updates as easy as possible in two ways: 1) We set up a calendar using Google Docs so teachers know in advance when their classes are up, and 2) We created a list of the steps students need to follow so they know what to anticipate. Typically, after the teachers select students, the group of children meets with the principal on Monday to go over the plan and then reconvenes later in the week to make the video when the children have gathered all the necessary information.

Step 5: Hone the vision.

As you build culture, continue to hone your vision of what that culture might become. Putting out fires and solving problems aren't enough to create an ideal school even when the systems you've put into place are thriving. Even a school with a strong positive culture can work on becoming a better iteration of itself. Enlist your "dream team" of students, teachers, and families to help hone the vision by generating a list of priorities for continued growth and revising the plan according to progress. Stasis leads to entropy in school culture as in nature. Breathe life into your school by keeping the culture vital and by seeking improvement.

OVERCOMING PUSHBACK

Even considering the significant influence an instructional lead learner has on creating a positive school culture, one cannot ignore the influence others have on the organization. Not everyone in the school may be supportive of the school leader's efforts to promote a positive school culture; in fact, some people may be intent on sabotaging it so it becomes divisive, negative, and potentially destructive.

Using social media to amplify school culture puts kids at risk. Social media usage is a hot topic in many schools and districts. Unfortunately, negative associations with social media cause hesitance about engaging with digital platforms. School leaders avoid social media because of concerns about everything from being publicly bashed to exposing students to online predators. Social media sites such as Twitter and Instagram conjure up thoughts of frivolous celebrities sharing minute-by-minute breakdowns of their daily activities, or worse, of well-publicized episodes of cyberbullying. The negative discourse around social media causes leaders to avoid it in many schools despite its obvious benefits.

Demystify the misconceptions that surround social media and consider the powerful opportunities these free resources offer to you as a school leader and to your community. Start by focusing on learning: Educate all members of the community about how the various social media platforms work and how to use them for positive purposes. For example, many schools have offered their staff voluntary training sessions on how to use social media sites. Because they know that knowledge is power, some school leaders have invited families in for Social Media 101 presentations to reframe their perceptions, allay their fears, and answer their questions. Finally, school leaders model appropriate digital citizenship by actively using social media for professional purposes, including developing a PLN for personal and professional development; creating a school hashtag to crowdsource information; and sharing pictures that demonstrate the importance of what happens in school.

Parents don't want their children on our social media stream. After sharing an outline of how you communicate with families using digital tools and social media, give families the opportunity to opt their children out if they are not comfortable having their pictures or stories used. Send a letter home explaining that in addition to the traditional media platforms such as newspapers and television news that might feature stories and pictures connected to the school, you are now integrating tools such as social media to accelerate and amplify the school story. If they don't want their children featured they must communicate that to you in writing. We have found that it is easier to handle families that may want to opt out as opposed to trying to get every family to sign off on a permission slip.

Staff morale is low and people are stressed out, so how can I broach the subject of C.U.L.T.U.R.E. with them? Even where there is a positive school culture, educators are constantly assailed by mandates that create stress and anxiety. Over the last several years we have seen this type of situation repeatedly when changes such as the Common Core Learning Standards or linking educator evaluations and high stakes test scores have made educators feel targeted, attacked, and disrespected. For many this is a daily reality, but that doesn't have to be the case.

Policies and mandates affect all schools, but school leaders determine how they manifest in the classroom and affect the educators. For example, a couple of years ago the New York State Education Department shared standardized instructional modules for English Language Arts on their EngageNY website. The materials weren't mandated by the state, so they didn't necessarily have to work their way into the classroom. Unfortunately, many school leaders took the availability of resources as a mandate and went online, printed out all the materials, created binders for the teachers, handed them out, and told the teachers to begin implementing the "curriculum" A.S.A.P. As one can imagine, this caused the morale in many schools to bottom out and school culture to spiral downward. There was no communication, there was no reflection—misinformed leaders made the decision irrespective of the impact.

This scenario does not have to reflect how we handle mandates and policies in our schools. Instead of lunging to implement policy changes, a transformational instructional lead learner will pause to review a policy's expectations and engage various community members on how it can be most meaningfully integrated into their school.

The keys to success are communication, reflection, and collaborative decision-making. If those techniques are employed, morale will remain high and culture will stay positive.

How can we increase test scores if we're focused on culture?
Culture and test scores don't have to be mutually exclusive. We can definitely focus on school culture and know that in the long term positive culture will have an impact on test scores. For example, we know that when children attend a school where they feel valued, confident, and happy, their brains release endorphins, which benefits their learning. When students are actively engaged in and have ownership of their learning, chances are they will perform well in all academic areas. Of course, this is only possible if the teachers are feeling similarly. To create a setting where students and teachers thrive and feel genuine joy, leaders must focus on school culture. The choice is yours: Get short-term results by investing in disconnected test prep activities, or lay the foundation for long-term results that can be transformational on many levels for years to come by investing in positive school culture.

THE HACK IN ACTION

Creating a vision statement is an integral step in communicating the school's C.U.L.T.U.R.E. But it is not necessarily an easy process that a leader can tackle in isolation.

Tony's Story

Revamping the Cantiague vision statement was something I had been struggling with for years because I wasn't quite sure about the best way to capture and represent our vision so that it clearly communicated the culture of Cantiague Elementary. So, three years ago our shared decision-making team of students, family members, and staff was charged with the important task of rewriting and recreating the school vision statement so it captured the essence of our culture. We wanted to amplify it so it reached far beyond the walls of our school.

We started by listing words that we felt best described Cantiague and the Cantiague experience. Generating that list, which ended up being about a hundred words and phrases, and then narrowing it down was quite a process. It involved surveys of staff, families, and kids; discussions; more surveys; and follow-up discussions. It took us months. After deciding on the words that best fit Cantiague we then shifted the conversation to what our vision statement should actually look like. Will we generate a bulleted list? Maybe we could write it in a different way? Should we go in a completely different direction and create a Wordle that would be permanently visible on our website? Although we engaged in rich discussion, we had a tough time coming to a conclusion.

The team kept coming back to the idea that a video might best capture the Cantiague experience. It would allow us to literally show our school vision using images of the life of the school. Thanks to the hard work of our team, the vision statement went from an idea to a video reality. We communicated what made us Cantiague, we uncovered the learning, we worked with transparency. Our vision statement was a true reflection of all that makes up our positive school C.U.L.T.U.R.E.

Although Tony's story about revamping the vision statement is specific to Cantiague, it speaks to the idea that any leader who wants to nurture and spread a positive school culture must build relationships that are rooted in trust and respect. These relationships are the impetus for effective communication, which is critical to school culture. We must be consistent and clear in communicating our sense of the culture to all members of the school. Creating a constant flow of information operates as a kind of formative assessment that will allow us to self-correct missteps and reinforce the best aspects of the school, leading to a durable and positive culture. School leaders who are transparent develop relational trust because communities respond to strong, consistent messages that are visible to everyone. Kids, families, and teachers will trust a school leader who helps them understand what he or she is doing and why, and who demonstrates actions that clearly serve the best interest of kids.

These relationships, high levels of trust, and cultural norms should then be communicated throughout the school and beyond it to ensure that the entire community shares a common vision. Be sure to clearly articulate the culture you want to create by rewriting and redefining the school vision statement. One of the first tasks given to those of us in a leadership position is to consider the vision statement for our school. You know what we are talking about: that bulleted list of generic phrases and words schools use to try and capture what the schooling experience will be like for its children. Here is an example, in case it's been a while since you looked at your own vision statement:

> Our vision is that children leave school with:
> A set of values—being honest, being determined, and being considerate of others.
> A set of basic skills—literate, mathematical, scientific, artistic, and social.
> Strong self-esteem and developed self-confidence. Tolerance and respect for others.
> We value the partnership which exists between school, families, and our community in realizing this vision.

Those sound like some pretty wonderful, important aspects of a child's development. But what is the point of this vision statement? What does it really mean for a school community? As you consider your school's C.U.L.T.U.R.E. make sure that it is undergirded by the school's vision statement, which should be personalized to your community and reflect common hopes, goals, and dreams for your students.

The school leader embodies a school's culture. Its leader's words and actions represent a school's priorities and concerns. We get a sense of culture when we witness a school leader:

- get down on the floor and smile while interacting with a group of first-graders,

- help a teacher navigate a difficult situation without passing judgment or controlling every aspect of the situation,

- patiently listen to and support an upset family member without reacting or getting defensive,

- take stakeholders' opinions into account when implementing policies.

We see a source of culture in the profound influence a school leader has on the community.

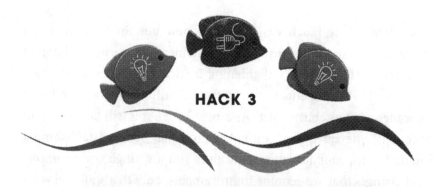

HACK 3

BUILD RELATIONSHIPS
Connect with intentionality

*Trust is the glue of life. It's the most essential
ingredient in effective communication. It's the
foundational principle that holds all relationships.*
—STEPHEN COVEY, AMERICAN AUTHOR, BUSINESSMAN

THE PROBLEM: LEADERS AREN'T DELIBERATE IN
THEIR APPROACH TO BUILDING RELATIONSHIPS

O LD WESTERN MOVIES are set in disreputable towns where chaos is the norm. There's no law, just people doing whatever they want and creating trouble around every turn. Inevitably, a new sheriff shows up with the intent to "clean up this town," and when he has completed the task he moves on to the next town to do the same. Some school leaders have this John Wayne mentality. They believe they are trouble-shooters whose job it is to clean up the "mess" that the last person left and get the group going in the right direction. The leadership challenge those new sheriffs never stuck around long enough to experience is to build relationships while sustaining positive change.

In reality, it is much easier for the new gun in town to build momentum than to sustain it. The excitement of hearing a different voice can initially feel so enlightening it triggers a honeymoon effect on the staff. This impetus to follow the new direction does not last if the leader can't establish trust. As a new leader you will be a different voice, but different doesn't automatically equal better. Establishing a foundation for sound relationships gives you a springboard to implement changes that are genuine improvements, ones that staff will want to sustain and build upon.

The importance of relationships in schools is indisputable. Whether you are a new leader, one that has been in the building for a few years, or a veteran administrator looking to reconnect with your staff, it is important to be deliberate when it comes to relationship building. Even though it's a commonplace truth that developing relationships is central to the overall culture of the building, we rarely discuss how to build those relationships.

We emphasize the centrality of relationships but don't specify deliberate practices to create or sustain them. If you have ever been to a youth sporting event you've probably seen firsthand the kind of misplaced emphasis we mean. Listen in on the advice a hard-core sport parent gives a kid who had less than stellar performance in a game: "You need to play harder."

We learn by doing, but we learn more by reflecting on what we have done.

How is the poor kid supposed to follow that command? Even if she has an intuitive sense of its importance, and perhaps a feel for what playing harder might be like, there's no real way to achieve success without more specific directions.

As educators, we've been trained to recognize the futility of this kind of vague feedback. If we had a student struggling with adding we would not advise him to work harder or get better at math, we would give that student specific practices to succeed. Sadly, our expertise in planning and scaffolding effective learning usually does not transfer into the way we approach interpersonal relationships.

Building relationships is about being intentional. Having said that, the hack will work only if it is born out of authenticity. If your attempts to build relationships are superficial or insincere, there is simply no book that can help.

THE HACK: BUILD RELATIONSHIPS

There is one silver bullet to moving schools forward: Be a model for both relationship building and learning. Being exceptional in these areas is key to success in any employment opportunity you may have as a school leader. The ability to cultivate relationships with stakeholders will allow a leader to develop and sustain momentum. Nurturing relationships will cost your organization zero dollars. The investment is in time.

Leadership programs that prepare future administrators devote much attention to the management side of schools. Scheduling, human resources, evaluations, and budget all warrant lengthy conversations. The importance of relationships is emphasized, but discussion rarely goes beyond that to deal with effective processes to forge and sustain those relationships. We suggest you take a more systematic approach to the relationship building by concentrating on two specific components: connect and reflect.

Connect. The *What You Can Do Tomorrow* and *Blueprint* sections of this hack provide a number of specific ways to connect with your staff. Strive to balance between real-time and virtual connections. If you always seek teachers in the classroom, they may get annoyed at the interruption. They will eventually wonder how you have enough time to be with them on such a consistent basis. Conversely, only connecting by sending positive notes, calls, and emails to people is not effective either. You don't want to give the impression that you hold people at a distance.

Reflect. We learn by doing, but we learn more by reflecting on what we have done. Being intentional about the process of building relationships also means being intentional about reflecting on how it works. During our initial years as administrators, we kept contact journals in our office. These were a fantastic way to see where we had been throughout the day and what parts of the building we had been missing. Presently, we use social media for reflection by scrolling through tweets at the end of the day to see where our journey has taken us. Being consistent in posting the great things happening in classrooms has made this reflection process much easier.

WHAT YOU CAN DO TOMORROW

- **Use Google for scheduling.** Set up a calendar with reminders to visit certain buildings or classrooms. Create a Google Form where people can share the great things going on in your building. This keeps you informed about what is happening in your space so you can see teachers do what they do best and validate their efforts. It also allows staff members to connect with their colleagues about great learning opportunities for kids.

- **Write positive notes.** Start your day by writing two positive notes to staff members. We suggest getting cards imprinted with your school logo, but any card will do. By starting your day writing a few positive notes, you are putting yourself in the right frame of mind. Jeff Zoul, Assistant Superintendent in Deerfield, Illinois, often remarks that writing a positive handwritten note to a staff member makes two people feel better: the staff member and the leader.

- **Conduct a hashtag review.** Take time each day to review your school or district hashtag on your social media channels so you can see what is going on in other classrooms. One of the easiest ways to do this is by setting up a notification system such as IFTTT to notify you via phone when the hashtag is used. For instance, when the hashtag #gocrickets is shared, IFTTT sends Joe a notification. This helps shine the light on the positive things happening, but can also allow you to circumvent problems if someone chooses to post something derogatory on your social media channels. Be sure to retweet and favorite exceptional practices so others can see them. Doing this shows your staff members that you value the work they do enough to send it to the world.

- **Follow through on all commitments.** As the leader of the building, you are moving in a number of different directions. Many of the conversations you have will take place in classrooms or hallways. Be sure to have a way to document the items you discuss so forgetting to follow up is never an issue. There are few things that destroy trust more than lack of follow-through with your staff members. If you say you are going to be in the building on a weekly basis, it is essential that you are there. If you are too busy to get into classrooms you need to adjust how your days flow to make more connections with staff and students. Staff are not going to feel like you're invested in your commitment to them if you become more visible only when you need people to serve on a committee or when a state official tasks you with a project. Scheduling opportunities to connect with staff members in and out of school is key to follow-through.

- **Make five positive phone calls about students to start or end your week.** This does a few things. First, it changes the lens through which you view everyday events. It is really easy to get sucked into what is going wrong at school, because the unfortunate truth is that negative stories take up a good deal of a leader's bandwidth. Knowing that you are going to start or end your week with calls to parents changes what you are looking for and helps your overall mentality when walking through the school. Second, it ensures that you are out of your office seeking out positive events and interactions. Visibility is a key to trust and your commitment to being with students and staff develops social capital. Finally, when your first contact with a parent is positive you create a positive home-to-school connection that will clearly help you in the long run.

- **Target issues appropriately.** Address issues immediately when they come up. Rather than making a blanket comment to the whole staff about an issue that really only involves a few people, deal with those individuals separately. Telling the whole room of educators to change their processes will backfire: Everyone knows who you are talking about, and they want you to address those involved instead of blaming the whole staff. Whereas some leaders think this is a gentler way of dealing with problems because people are not singled out, the staff will resent being lumped in with the wrong-doers and perceive that you are too weak to address issues one-on-one so they actually get resolved. Most staff are doing the right work, their best work, and when others don't it devalues their own. For example, if you are collecting planbooks and only three teachers haven't handed them in, don't email the whole staff a reminder—just ask those specific people to submit their plans.

* **Send cards to family members.** Being a teacher or a staff member in a school can be extremely draining to those around you. We often forget that the people we work with go home to an entirely different life, one they need to tend to so everyone stays happy. How often do we say thank you to those who help our staff members get through tough times with students, colleagues, and yes, even administrators? Taking the time to write and mail a quick note to the spouse, children, or parents of your staff members shows you value your staff and their support systems. The reaction of spouses and families is astounding. We can't even begin to tell you how many times we have been stopped by families of our staff members so they can thank us. The notes were quick, but the reaction has been extremely beneficial. Such small gestures forge trusting interpersonal bonds.

A BLUEPRINT FOR FULL IMPLEMENTATION

Step 1: Build up momentum before the school year starts.

The summer is a great time to start building momentum for the school year. Though you don't want to send the proverbial "back to school letter" in June, you can be thinking of ways to make people feel great about returning to school.

- **Call the teachers.** We make personal phone calls to staff members the night before the first day back. Nothing fancy, we just use the opportunity to chat and see how they are feeling about the upcoming year. A summer away from school is a great reason for you to reconnect and set the scene for the upcoming year. The first time we did this, teachers reacted the same way as parents did when teachers began making positive calls. They often stopped the conversation to wonder what was wrong. By the third year they were wondering what took so long to get to their name.

- **Provide back-to-school swag.** People love new school gear. Before the staff exits for the year be sure to get their t-shirt sizes so you can have a small care package ready for each of them when they arrive back on campus. We try to make the shirts relatively general without an annual theme, but some groups enjoy the focus of a yearly vision. Having identical clothing serves the same purpose as it does on the sports field: It labels each individual as part of a cohesive group, creating a sense of belonging and identifying everyone as a team member.

Step 2: Ditch the opening staff meeting.

We hate to be the bearers of bad news, but your staff does not want to hear you speak at great length on opening day. The knowledge that in less than a week their classrooms will be filled with bodies means that their minds are focused elsewhere. Keep the message motivating and *short*! The social capital you will build with them is far better than anything you have to say on the first day. Give them the information you must disseminate in other ways:

- Set up a folder on a shared drive that has all of the information needed to start the year. They can reference it as needed.

- Create a ten-minute video that introduces any district needs that are rich in information but not urgent. This will give staff an opportunity to view it at their leisure and reference it throughout the year.

Step 3: Find places to celebrate the efforts of staff members.
Ask kids and staff members for permission to share their work with other groups.

- Start every school board meeting with a student highlight to allow staff and students to show off an achievement or activity. Staff members will be happy to invite you back to their rooms when they see you walking away excited about a specific activity idea that they hold dear. Remembering that activity will give you a specific talking point when you see them again. When you validate their efforts by sharing their work with others, you prove how much you value them.

- Contact local media to celebrate staff efforts. Being extremely positive with your local media will land you great coverage of your school. You may not get everything in the paper or on the news, but the mere fact that you are giving them information will have a profound impact on how they view and present you.

- The school newspaper is not dead. Remember that the vast majority of your local community does not have kids in school but they still want to be connected. While we would contend that Facebook reaches the most people, community members still enjoy seeing a quarterly newspaper. It affords them the opportunity to reminisce about a time when they had kids in school or were in school themselves. Sending these to alumni also helps you spread the word across the country and even has a global impact.

Step 4: Meet the staff where they like to be.

Finding ways to connect outside of school can be a fantastic way to develop relationships with your staff. Throughout the course of a 190-contracted-day school year the people in your building will spend over 1,500 hours of time together. In a larger school, teachers may have very little contact with each other for most of those hours because they are all busy in their own separate spaces. Having the opportunity to talk off site gives your staff members a chance to connect in a new place and see people they don't often get a chance to interact with.

> You build culture every time you walk down the hallway, every time you bend down to help a student tie a shoe, every time you walk into a classroom to have a heartfelt conversation with a staff member.

Offering multiple possibilities for event venues is essential as people have different comfort zones when it comes to getting together outside of school. Ask them what they prefer. Some people like to go to a local eatery after school together, some people like to attend a school athletic event, some people like to have a potluck dinner at a colleague's home. You are responsible for the needs of your staff; diversifying the opportunities you give people to connect will allow you to touch the greatest number of them. Meeting people where they feel comfortable is a great way to have everyone invest in the process of moving forward.

Step 5: Participate in the big events.

Throughout the course of the year a number of events celebrate the work of students and educators across the world. Be ready to make your school shine on those particular days.

- **100 Calls on the 100th Day.** On the 100th day of school, take the advice of elementary school principal Melissa Kartsimas and make 100 calls to the parents of 100 students. Prior to the 100th day send out a Google Form to your staff and ask for suggestions for specific things students have done recently that made them smile. The form can simply ask for the teacher's name, student's name, and what the student did to provoke a smile. Sharing this information with parents connects you to them, but also emphasizes that the teacher saw something exceptional in their child.

- **The Personal Day Giveaway.** In Deerfield, Illinois, the central office administrative cabinet raffles off a number of personal days for their staff members during the week before winter break. Staff members are allowed to take a personal day while the central office personnel cover the class or designated area for the day. It costs the district nothing and boosts everyone's morale. The Personal Day Giveaway is now a tradition in Fall Creek as well.

Step 6: Take advantage of the small events.

Relationships are constructed in every interaction. People tend to excuse relationship breakdown by claiming not to have enough time to nurture it properly. Try this exercise the next time you are with your best friend. Sit two feet from him/her and stare at each other for thirty seconds without either of you saying a word. You will honestly think that your watch stopped. Thirty seconds is all you need to get your foot in the door with your staff. The approach we need to take is we *have* thirty seconds, not we *only* have thirty seconds. You can build relationships in small events throughout the year that will build trust and capacity with your group. Here are a few to try:

- **Take a classroom.** Be the person to cover classrooms when needed, or when not needed. Send out an email saying, "Hey everyone! I'm walking around school this morning. If you need fifteen minutes for a break let me know and I'll pop in!" You'll get a huge response. After your time is fully booked send out another email indicating you are filled up, but will definitely do it again soon.

- **Take the school.** Yep, you read that right. Take the school for a forty-five-minute block periodically so your staff can have uninterrupted planning time with colleagues. You can take the kids through team-building games or have an all-school assembly. If your school is on the larger side, divide it into smaller groups and assign each member of the administrative team a group so everyone is part of the experience. The staff will truly appreciate your efforts.

- **Surprise the staff.** For those of you who live where there is snow, head out to the parking lot with your administrative team on a day when cars are snow-covered and brush off windshields and lights. Your staff will be delighted with the after-school surprise.

Step 7: Be transparent about your growth.

Feedback is an essential part of progress. Great leaders provide authentic feedback to their groups in both formal and informal capacities. Show your commitment to your own development by asking your staff to offer you feedback so you can grow. Making this process transparent helps develop trust with your group. Break down the feedback walls by implementing the following tips:

- Use a Google Form—and keep it short. We suggest conducting two quick surveys, one in the middle of the school year and one at the end. Keeping the form short is essential as both of those times are busy for staff members.

- Once the form is complete and the data is collected find two things that are going well and develop a two-step plan for each to keep the momentum going. Find one thing that is not going well and develop a two-step plan to improve that area.

- Post the data and the plan in the staff lounge and send it to all staff members. This takes a great deal of vulnerability, but the payoff is worth it. Your staff will respect the fact that you are addressing needs and know that you are working on specific pieces of your leadership ability.

OVERCOMING PUSHBACK

Building capacity and creating time are the best ways to sustain momentum and help people who are set on pushing back ideas that will move the group forward. Identifying what roles people play in your organization will help you to amplify the voices of your opinion leaders.

You can't force relationships. True. Think back to anyone you have had a connection with in the past. You almost certainly had interests in common, since we tend to gravitate toward people who share our mindset and concerns. This happens in school as well. Staff members connect with people who share an affinity with them and veer from those who do not. Using a systematic approach to connections is not intended to make you the best friend of everyone on your staff. Rather, it is a way to open the door to conversations that are built around a common interest: the desire to have a favorable work environment.

If you do this for everyone it doesn't feel genuine. You'll connect with some staff members more than with others. Your kids may be the same age, you may have attended the same college, or you may cheer for the same professional sports team. In other cases, you may have to work a bit harder to find those connections. Being intentional does not mean being insincere. This hack is intended to help you to understand where staff members are coming from so you can find a connection with everyone in your school community.

I just want you to be my boss, that's it. Let's be clear about one thing: There will likely be those in your organization who are not excited about your guidance. Often it is because they don't align to the direction they believe you are leading people. It may be because they don't want to change their processes, they feel comfortable in their space, or they simply don't connect with you. Though this is unfortunate, we stress getting to know people for a reason. The more opportunities you have had to connect with those who are not on the train, the better the chances are that you will be able to sit down and hold a discussion with them in a professional manner.

A private chat can be a fantastic way to deal with naysayers because they tend to be loud. They want people to know that they are opposed and will start conversations with colleagues in the lounge regarding anything and everything happening in the building. Reaching out to them and meeting them where they are can be immensely beneficial.

Making a personal connection usually eliminates personal attacks and then you can get to a conversation that is about the direction of the building. They will (not may, *will*) have legitimate concerns about your leadership. Others may share those concerns but not feel comfortable speaking out, and therefore you may not hear about them often.

THE HACK IN ACTION

Jimmy Casas is the principal at Bettendorf High School in Bettendorf, Iowa. He is the 2012 Iowa State Principal of the Year and one of three finalists for National Principal of the Year in 2013. Jimmy knows the importance of relationships and stresses this in his building on a regular basis. Bettendorf operates under a culture of excellence model where everyone is responsible for upholding high standards in all areas of the building.

That is not to say that Jimmy's building is without issues. When a situation arises where a staff member is struggling, he finds a way to meet them where they are and celebrate what they contribute to that culture. He then asks the staff member to commit to doing something in their strength zone that can help another member of the school community. This increases the confidence level of the staff member, but also develops trust in Jimmy as the leader.

Because he has built these relationships with a number of people in the school, he has a reservoir of people who can help when staff members have an issue. Jimmy can address the need by partnering the staff member with someone in the building who is doing exceptional work in that particular area. The struggling staff member can be an expert in one area and struggle in another, but in either case he or she gets connected to others so people can learn and grow together.

Building relationships takes time, and there are days that you will feel like you have none. Dealing with all the things on your plate and the day-to-day operations of school can get overwhelming. However, if you think about relationship building in small increments, the idea is much easier to fathom. Every interaction with your staff shapes the culture of your building. You build culture every time you walk down the hallway, every time you bend down to help a student tie a shoe, every time you walk into a classroom to have a heartfelt conversation with a staff member. The building leader has a profound impact on the learning environment. We will get what we model in all areas of our work.

FLATTEN THE WALLS OF YOUR SCHOOL
Create partnership with the community

*Storytelling is the most powerful way to
put ideas into the world today.*
—ROBERT MCAFEE BROWN, THEOLOGIAN AND CIVIL RIGHTS ACTIVIST

THE PROBLEM: IN THE ABSENCE OF KNOWLEDGE, PEOPLE MAKE THEIR OWN TRUTH

Joe's Story

WHEN I WAS in first grade, a crew of neighborhood kids would pick me up for school every day. They were a fantastic group of elementary students in grades 3-6. We would walk together to school, and they would make sure I got to the playground safely. They also shepherded me home at the end of the day. During the school day, most of the classroom interactions I witnessed were between students and teachers. My parents went to school for a few reasons: to pick me up when I was sick, to attend parent/teacher conferences, to support disciplinary action if I ended up in the principal's office. Thankfully, the latter only happened on a few occasions. For the most part I was a good kid who did average work, so there were not many reasons for my parents to be in the school. My parents usually had three to five on-site connections to our school building a year.

This separation between home and school remains the norm in many schools, prolonging the notion that families and educators are not there for each other. Parents drop off their kids at school and then pick them up at the end of the day, hoping they had a good experience but not really knowing what happened. The impression parents have of their child's school day gets conflated with their own school experience. When they think about school, they inevitably remember what school was like when they were there, which was not always positive. For these parents, the propensity to think about what went wrong and throw blame sometimes comes more readily than to celebrate the positive aspects of their school days. If we are to rely on our parents and community members to help us change that narrative, then it is incumbent upon us to give them the tools to do so.

Flattening the walls of your school entails eliminating the communication barriers so everyone feels like they are part of the school community.

Educators who are highly transparent tend to engage students, parents, and colleagues because they are often powerful storytellers. Assuming it is authentic stuff—remember, the brand experience must match the brand promise—their narratives tend to resonate with people because what they share is consistent and visible to all. Their messages originate in beliefs and non-negotiable priorities that are in the best interest of children. Transparency can therefore develop relational trust. Kids, families, and colleagues will trust you if they know what you are doing, why you are doing it, and that it is best for kids.

Educators who develop trusting relationships with their communities build a significant amount of social capital, and that is a gold mine. When we amass social capital we have the foundation for enacting change, trying new things, and telling our school stories. Having trusting relationships at the core of a community allows educators a degree of risk-taking that would not be possible otherwise.

Tools such as Twitter, Instagram, and Facebook offer significant possibilities for telling our stories and branding our spaces. Technology allows us to amplify our school story beyond the walls of our school and accelerate the development of healthy relationships within our community and beyond. Likewise, pictures of students and staff in action engage an audience, transforming us from sources of information to storytellers. Our narratives mold our community, which in turn shape the narrative about our schools and contribute to increasingly healthy relationships.

We implore our fellow educators to embrace the notion of being highly transparent because transparency leads to trust, which helps build social capital, which must be in place to effect transformation.

THE HACK: FLATTEN THE WALLS

In an age where information is readily available to anyone at any time, we can leverage communication channels to break down the school-as-fortress attitude and move to support each other for the benefit of our kids. Flattening the walls of your school entails eliminating the communication barriers so everyone feels like they are part of the school community. Create C.U.L.T.U.R.E. that incorporates all members of the community, including students, families, and educators. Everyone in the community should have access to the learning occurring in school, and that begins by knocking down walls and stepping over boundaries to transform from fortress to partnership. This requires a shift in practice, but also a shift in philosophy so that educators view engaging with students and their families as an opportunity rather than a challenge.

WHAT YOU CAN DO TOMORROW

- **Find out where stakeholders spend their virtual lives.** Survey school families about their online preferences. To reach everyone, send both electronic and paper copies. This will give you a quick look at their online lives. Based on national trends you will find adults on Facebook, students on Instagram, and a collection of both on Twitter. Those will probably be your three areas of focus. When you decide on the tools you will use, take the time to come up with a handle (username) that is unique to the school.

- **Create a calendar.** Make a list of all the great things that are happening in your school that you could add to your Twitter and Facebook feeds. Our guess is that you can come up with 15-20 immediately. Once you have a list, add each item to a calendar such as Google Calendar. This way when you get to school you already have ideas for what to post that day. Add reminders on your calendar to post great things happening in your building, such as kids playing on the playground, a fantastic lunchroom, new spaces for learning, or collaborative group work.

- **Leverage the power of the hashtag.** A Twitter hashtag is a superb tool that allows anyone to get involved with your school's narrative on Twitter and other social media. Using a hashtag helps students and staff to exercise their voices on their terms. People can still have individual accounts and use the hashtag to filter any school-related thoughts to the school's collective narrative just by typing a few characters. When Joe arrived at Fall Creek, he visited a local museum and found a variety of "Go Crickets" memorabilia and decided to embrace the "Go Crickets" mantra as a way of building community. Soon, the #gocrickets Twitter feed sprang to life with daily tweets about Fall Creek Cricket life. Now, the #gocrickets Twitter feed streams directly to the main school website and scrolls on large screens throughout the K-12 building daily so everyone in school can see the amazing things happening every day. The hashtag is the key.

A BLUEPRINT FOR FULL IMPLEMENTATION

Step 1: Connect online tools for ease of use.

One of the fears we hear from administrators about engaging in social media is that it adds one more thing to an already full plate. Efficiency may help cut the load. Connecting platforms makes the work of posting in multiple areas easier. Facebook and Twitter both offer linking options so every time you post to Twitter it shows up in your Facebook feed. You can also use a number of different third-party services to automate the work. These tools allow you to direct different platforms from one control station so you can post to multiple areas.

Step 2: Set goals for communication.

Stagnant social media channels crush the flow of storytelling in your space. Juggling between communicating too much and not enough can be difficult, and the balance usually depends on your community.

The goal of the Fall Creek School District is to have at least seven positive posts per week about activities other than athletics.

Step 3: Plan the roll-out.

Launching your social media channels is a fantastic feeling! Once you have a handle and hashtag, start getting the word out. First, email your distribution lists a message announcing the new forums you will use to celebrate your space. Let everyone know exactly what you will be using social media for and what behaviors will not be tolerated. The social media flow should go both ways, communicating information and celebrations from families as well as staff. Emphasize that the messages are opportunities to celebrate the work and not a sounding board for negativity.

Now it's time to launch. The best way to get people involved is to win them over quickly. Think about it like this: communicate a great story, evoke emotion, follow up with leverage. Find the most amazing thing about your school—ensure it is a story that involves staff and students. As you think about the form your post will take, understand that visuals create an emotional connection. Posting "We love it when our kids work collaboratively!" is great, but a picture of kids working collaboratively will evoke stronger reactions from your community. Make events a huge deal. Call the local media so they know something is happening, and post it to your social media channels in real time. When it is over, use the email distribution lists you have created to share the story with everyone. Your engagement on those pages will go through the roof.

Step 4: Keep the momentum rolling.

Now that you have people watching your space, you need to keep them there. You will have an initial phase where much attention gets focused on the platforms. Figure out what people are enjoying about your posts so you can maintain this attention.

One of the benefits of using social media channels is how much it changes the conversations at home. Giving parents specific things to talk to their children about instead of asking, "What did you do in school today?" will evoke a much more substantial response than the typical "Nothing." Gaining knowledge empowers parents, so they will go back for more information. Continuing to feed that bank of knowledge keeps the momentum going with your platforms. Here are a few ways to send the message to parents in your school:

- Parents may not have a social media account, but most have access to the Internet. Streaming your Twitter and/or Facebook feed on the main page of your school website will help parents find the amazing things happening in your school.

- Give control of the social media account to a student for the day and make contact with the parents prior to the student taking it over. Word of mouth is still incredibly powerful and if parents know that their child is running the feed, they'll make sure people hear about it. This also motivates and sets a level of expectation for the student as he or she will know parents are watching.

- Use a service that collates your tweets. Apps such as Storify allow you to create a social media story that can be shared with parents via email or printed off and sent home for those who do not have Internet access.

- Contests can feed the momentum. Publish a post on your page announcing that the first five people who find you at a football game or music concert and tell you the vision of the school district will get a school t-shirt. Post a picture of a sticker with a school mascot on it somewhere in the school and tell kids that the first person to reply on Facebook, Twitter, or Instagram indicating where it is will get a $10 gift certificate and a t-shirt. Contests drive people to your communication platforms and ensure that the conversation about school is continuous.

OVERCOMING PUSHBACK

The pushback for opening a school to the world is often founded in fear of something going wrong. The potential for something negative to appear on your social media platforms is real and can definitely be scary. As a leader you will need to address this fear with three groups of people: staff, parents, and supervisors. Make the potential benefits of using social media clear to all three groups. Highlighting the positive eliminates much of the pushback from these groups.

Teachers are going to complain that this is one more addition to their already overcrowded agendas. We don't see keeping stakeholders informed as something that should add more time to an educator's day, we see it as such a priority that educators need to adjust their time to include it. Interacting with parents and community members is essential to the growth of your school and district: You need people on your side. Conversations with staff should focus less on buying in than on building momentum. Current narratives about public education are more Charles Dickens than Pollyanna Sunshine, and the more people we can get talking about the great things happening in schools, the better off we all are. If your people are not on board, the initiative will founder. Start with them, even before you move to parents and your supervisors.

This is a tough sell to the superintendent. Go to the district office prepared with evidence proving the value of the initiative and with a clear plan to deal with eventualities. Your superintendent has a personal stake in your activity: He or she needs to answer to someone if it goes wrong. District administrators have to justify decisions to a group of people who may all have different reasons for being on the school board. The board needs to know how a new direction is going to benefit them and the people they represent. If you have a groundswell of support in your building it is much more likely that the district administrator and board will support it.

THE HACK IN ACTION

In 2011, the Fall Creek School District unveiled its Facebook page and Twitter account. Prior to the launch they surveyed the community to see which platforms people used most frequently. They reviewed the policy regarding student images and identification to create a process and policy to guide staff members. In the first week of school the administration team set up an event that they knew would get some local media coverage.

While the Fall Creek staff was in a meeting, the administrators rolled out a red carpet outside the meeting room, set up a rope barrier on either side, and had thirty kids sneak into position. As the surprised staff members exited the meeting they were met by thirty screaming students who were taking pictures and asking for autographs. It was the Oscars—in Fall Creek, Wisconsin. The local news broadcast the event, and the Facebook page lit up. Thousands of likes and shares within a day landed the story on the "Daily Best" of CNN.com. The great story, emotion, and leverage made the launch extremely successful.

The emotion elicited by school sports can also build a passionate audience. In the spring of 2013, Fall Creek Alumnus Dave Strasburg approached Joe about the prospect of putting a Fall Creek sports anthology on our website. He had pictures, audio, and video of Fall Creek sports highlights dating back to 1917. The collection was amazing. Footage of state basketball championships, school records, interviews with coaches and players, all shouting the pride of Fall Creek schools.

Dave was not a district employee. It would have been very easy, but divisive, to insist on controlling the message Dave wanted to disseminate. Joe had only been principal in Fall Creek for a year and knew Dave as the public address announcer, but that was really about it. After a conversation about all of the artifacts Dave had at his disposal, they decided to start a Facebook page that chronicled the great things that have happened over the course of the past eighty years. Once they negotiated the parameters for linking to the page on the district website, the project was entirely under Dave's control.

Since 2013 the page has become the "go to" for all things Fall Creek Athletics. What was intended as a page dedicated to the history of Fall Creek sports now includes stories, updates, and scores for past, current, and future Crickets. The page highlights high school athletics, middle school athletics, youth programs, coaches, all with the intent to celebrate the great things happening in Fall Creek. Dave has crowdsourced by including multiple parents as administrators. They know and understand what can and can't go on the page and have done a remarkable job of telling the school's story through Facebook. The page has as many likes as the district page. Dave and his parent volunteers truly know what it means to be Crickets and do a wonderful job of tapping into the pride of the community.

Telling a school's story shapes its culture, giving individuals a common identity as members of the school community. When a leader elects to become the chief storyteller, to celebrate the school's successes, focus shifts away from the school being a disciplinary institution or training facility to rejoice in its status as a learning community. Making the school walls transparent will transform both your school and your community.

HACK 5

BROADCAST STUDENT VOICES
Appeal to your audience to generate support

*A lack of transparency results in distrust
and a deep sense of insecurity.*
—Tenzin Gyatso, Dalai Lama

THE PROBLEM: SCHOOLS ARE REACTIVE

SCHOOL LEADERS SPEND a great deal of time defending decisions. *Where does the money go? Why did you implement that curriculum? What's the deal with school lunch?* Administrators have sometimes referred to the public's view of what's important about school as the three B's: beans, buses, and balls. If it concerns food (beans), transportation (buses), or athletics (balls), the administrator is going to hear about it. Many district administrators spend more time daily talking to the public about these three issues than about the education of students.

We can complain about that, or we can leverage the passion that the three B's evoke to connect with our families and gather some momentum in other areas. Being proactive in all aspects of schooling should be the default, but addressing the community's hot button topics can get people moving in the right direction.

Families want to know what is going on in our classrooms and schools. If we choose to believe that everything that happens in school is solely the responsibility of the educators and everything that happens outside of school is solely the responsibility of the families, then we are perpetuating a fortress mentality that can be counterproductive to our students' education.

> **The impact of hearing a student's voice expressing excitement over what the class learned in school can transform everyone involved.**

Becoming a partnership school can transform the entire community. Partnership schools elevate transparency and trust to norms; they recognize collaboration between home and school as crucial to success. Everyone is a valued contributor and participant in the learning experiences and culture of the school community.

THE HACK: BROADCAST STUDENT VOICES

The idea here is to forge community connections using a narrative. Television networks are masters at this. They know how to leverage our desire for connection to others. In 2016 networks arranged for the Super Bowl television coverage to start six hours before kickoff. They used all of that time to tell stories about the participants, exercising those narratives to make connections to the audience. With only two teams playing, there were a number of fan bases that didn't have an emotional connection to the teams on the field. To create that connection, the networks presented stories that tugged at the audience's emotions. You might not have been interested in the teams playing the game, but you made an emotional connection to one of the players. Audiences were hooked into the game as a result.

The community needs very little encouragement to be invested in its beloved school children; family and neighborhood bonds tie them together naturally. Having students present narratives about their education will eliminate the perception that there is an invisible divide that separates home and school into entirely independent spaces. Because these narratives are compelling just on the strength of the community's emotional ties to the children, they will forge more connections between school and the community than you ever thought possible.

WHAT YOU CAN DO TOMORROW

Use tech tools to amplify student voices. Kids say and do amazing things in school and parents are rarely around to witness them. Logistically, many teachers (elementary, in particular) spend more time with children during the weekday than their parents do. Parents and community members have a desire to connect with what is happening in your building. Putting a few tech tools into use tomorrow can help you connect with them right away.

- **Teach kids to podcast.** The voices of kids can and should be powerful in your school community. Parents love to hear them, community members remember what it was like to be them, and teachers can celebrate the great things happening in their classrooms without feeling like they are always defending their practice. Podcasts can powerfully amplify students' voices because they allow you to send information about your school to users in a medium that they already use. Don't be fooled into thinking you have to create some sort of elaborate process to put a podcast together. You can literally start podcasting tomorrow using a platform such as Spreaker.

- **Send out a live stream.** We live in a world where everything can be documented from a phone or portable device. Live streaming apps like Periscope and Meerkat allow you to broadcast anything from your school or classroom from the palm of your hand. Embracing those tools means that the dynamics of the classroom can be sent out for the world to see in seconds. Live streaming has made school events visible to the world: sports, concerts, and school plays can be recorded in real time. That may be scary for staff members. Conversely, it can show a level of transparency that we have never seen in schools before. Take advantage of live streaming to film a live debate, Periscope a presentation for parents who want to see the culmination of their child's hard work, or connect with a student who is homebound.

A BLUEPRINT FOR FULL IMPLEMENTATION

Step 1: Find your people.

Locating your audience's preferred virtual domains can focus your broadcasts. Send a simple survey at the beginning and end of each school year to ask people which social media platforms they use. This will help you avoid shouting to an empty room. We have found our families on Facebook and Twitter. Even if we provide an alternate platform for broadcasting we tend to promote it through channels we know our people use, and these often change over the course of a school year.

Step 2: Make the process easy.

We want to make sure the voices of students get to the community, but we don't want to make the process so taxing that teachers and students shy away from it. Make broadcasting easy so you don't wind up seeing the same few people celebrating the same events all the time. All you need to organize the staff posts is a Google Form with a contact name, the activity, and the best time to connect. You could also attach your Google Form as a link on your email signature so it is accessible to people in and out of your school community. Make accessing the posts easy as well. Think about how many emails you send in a day. Consider how many hits your broadcasts could have if each of those emails had a link that gave people easy access to your school celebrations.

Step 3: Empower others.

There will be times throughout the year that the craziness of school leadership takes over. Before it gets to that point think about people who can help and allow them to be part of the process from the start. We tend to ask, not assign when we'd like help. If someone is willing to get stories to the community, find a way to take something off of her plate so it doesn't feel like a burden. You can cover a recess duty, take over a class, or arrange for her to leave work before the end of the day so she can do the additional work. This costs zero dollars and can help people feel valued.

Step 4: Ease into it.

At first the desire to broadcast everything may take over. This honeymoon phase could result in a tremendous amount of content pushed out in the first couple of weeks. Then when you are settled in you may realize that you need to pull back to focus on other things that demand your time. Finding time is a challenge, but one you won't regret. Set a goal to keep a consistent social media feed and commit to adding a few posts daily. This won't be overwhelming. It will also help you focus on the positive things happening in your school.

OVERCOMING PUSHBACK

This is going to open me up for trouble. The community, the parents, and the board do not want to get surprised by anything that happens in school. Inevitably, problems will happen, but creating relationships is worth the risk. Being proactive should be the default any time you connect with people outside of the building. The connections your podcasts make between home and school are instrumental in developing social capital so you have support when things go awry.

People will say I'm just a publicity hound who is exploiting the kids for my own benefit. Make it clear to naysayers that your purpose for podcasting is not initiatives, money, or publicity. It is to share real school stories that touch the public's emotions. People identify with those stories. The impact of hearing a student's voice expressing excitement over what the class learned in school can transform everyone involved. The student has an opportunity to express learning beyond the teacher to the outside world. For the teacher it serves as formative assessment, a check for understanding. Finally, the impact on the community is substantial.

We want our community to be involved with the school, but we realize that people cannot get into our building on a regular basis. Hearing the voice of a student who has discovered something new may create a buzz around the wonderful work happening in schools. We send podcasts out on a regular basis so our board members stay in tune with school events. They work full-time jobs, yet want to be involved. Listening to podcasts on their own time allows them to connect with the school and then follow up with a note or a call. A sense of trust and recognition of value ensue when all staff members know that the school board is paying attention to their classrooms. When our board members reach out and can elaborate on specific practices happening in school it makes everyone feel like they are pulling in the same direction.

THE HACK IN ACTION

We build trust by offering knowledge. Families feel much more confident in the quality of education their children are getting when they understand what happens in the school. Once they hear school narratives in their own children's voices they will want to take part in celebrating your successes. Understanding your purposes and methods will convert them to champions who help build your momentum. Broadcasting your everyday school stories knits the community together in a common identity.

Penngrove Elementary School Principal and CUE Site Leader of the Year, Amy Fadeji, harnesses the power of podcasts and videocasts to publicize the amazing things happening in her school. Her Panther VP (Video Production) Crew, consisting of fourth through sixth graders, produces *The Penn News*, a weekly show that informs parents and students about the wonderful things happening on campus. The newscasts are completely student-driven.

Amy can also be found on the playground regularly, capturing student voice through the podcasting app audioBoom. Walking up to a group of students playing a game or having a conversation sometimes turns into a five-minute podcast that she can share with the world immediately. audioBoom affords her the opportunity to record and publish from one platform. Broadcasting real voices in real time has certainly helped Penngrove gain momentum.

When we only communicate sporadically or limit communication to polished "PR spots" we give the impression that we only connect with the community when we need something. Our ultimate purpose in telling school stories is not to self-promote or to guilt community members into being more actively involved in the school; our aim is to surround our children with trusting, nurturing, collaborative adults who prove they value education by paying attention to it, by committing to improve it. We must therefore acknowledge the truth of what happens every single day in our schools. We are better together, and being transparent with our community is essential for that partnership.

HACK 6

CENTER SCHOOL AROUND THE CHILDREN

Create schools that work for kids

Wisdom begins in wonder.
—SOCRATES, TEACHER AND PHILOSOPHER

THE PROBLEM: WE SET SCHOOLS UP FOR ADULTS, NOT FOR KIDS

THINK ABOUT YOUR conversations with other educators: When you talk about school, which topics dominate? If your conversations are anything like ours, you talk about teaching and learning, and the teaching predominates. When teachers dive more deeply into conversation they discuss topics like educator evaluations, high stakes standardized testing, and the current landscape of education. Leaders' exchanges often involve challenges related to negotiating contracts, dealing with staffing issues, or tackling the realities of enhancing instruction with limited resources. Invariably, our discussions focus on the concerns of the adults in the system rather than the learning of the children. Just as teaching dominates our conversations, the needs of adults generally take precedence over those of the children in a school.

Of course children are definitely a priority in schools across the country, but when we consider the way schools traditionally work, it is safe to say that most are adult-centered. Adults make the decisions about instruction, teaching, and learning. Customarily, adults allocate the budget, lead the meetings, facilitate the learning, and determine the school-wide practices. Even concerning issues such as classroom set-up and the flow of the day where the children are arguably more invested than the grown-ups, no one solicits students' opinions. School experiences revolve around the building's adults. They feel justified in driving the decisions and actions because that's the way it always has been done.

When we create schools that work for kids, the tone of discourse about learning changes so opportunities to innovate, create, and pursue passions become the norm rather than the exception.

In an adult-centric education system, those with the power—the adults—sometimes put initiatives into place that seem counterproductive to the purposes of learning just because they are not taking into account the learners they serve. During a recent conversation with a group of school leaders about literacy instruction, one principal shared that her district had adopted a scripted basal program, which made those of us who use a balanced literacy approach gasp in shock. She explained that her district felt the scripted basal program would be easier for teachers to implement based on their complaints about the difficulty and open-endedness of the balanced literacy model. They also believed it would help standardize instruction across the district.

So, regardless of the best interest of children, the impetus for the change was to pacify the adults and make the teaching easier. We can all think of dozens of situations like this one, where making things easier for the educators took priority over striving toward a student-centered learning community. Children often lack voice and choice in what occurs throughout the day because adults organize education according to their own priorities.

THE HACK: SITUATE THE SCHOOL'S POWER IN THE KIDS

The goal for every school should be to become a student-centered learning community that functions as a safe haven for children. When children feel safe, they feel confident; when children feel confident, they feel happy; when children feel happy, their brains release endorphins; when their brains release endorphins, children are primed for learning. A student-centered school pivots around the core philosophy that schools foster happy, engaged children who have voice in their learning and choice in how to communicate their knowledge. Students need to be active members of the school community. How that looks will depend on the school, but we need to shift the focus from the adults to spotlight the children.

Several essential components form a solid foundation for any student-centered school. Children need to view the school's adults as nurturing collaborators. To that end, we must prove to them that educators will support them and at the same time push them to learn and grow. Students need to believe that educators will advocate for them, that they will be just rather than exacting arbitrary punishment. Sometimes this means adults will motivate students when they cannot motivate themselves and help them develop all aspects of themselves. Adults must communicate these messages consistently. Children in a school should feel confident that their educators love (or at least like) and respect them.

In any school that genuinely focuses on learning, children appreciate the purpose of their learning experiences. Children want to understand the point of the work they are doing in school; they learn best when they perceive school work as appealing and valuable. If we embrace a hacker mindset and shift the focus away from the adults, we nurture an environment where whatever is being taught matters to kids. School will thus empower students with knowledge that will contribute positively to their lives.

When we create schools that work for kids, the tone of discourse about learning changes so opportunities to innovate, create, and pursue passions become the norm rather than the exception. Opportunities like Brilliance Builder—our take on a combined Makerspace and Genius Hour experience—become reality and children direct their own learning while they develop the 21st century skills of critical thinking, creating, collaborating, and communicating.

But why stop there? Children could participate in all school-wide decisions, from planning special events to sitting on interview committees for new teachers. When students exercise their voices, they position themselves as partners in their school experiences. If children are truly the priority, we should ensure that their involvement percolates through the whole school. We need to harness the excitement and enthusiasm our children bring to school each day, amplify their voices, and let their positivity permeate the entire community.

 WHAT YOU CAN DO TOMORROW

Creating a school that works for kids requires that we de-center adult needs and priorities to foreground those of our students. Our kids come to school with a wealth of knowledge, experience, and ability—let's access that potential and trust our children with opportunities to be lead learners. Our kids are not empty vessels to be filled with information: They need direct personal experiences to evolve, grow, and learn.

- **Ask for input.** Before you decide how you want to give students a voice in your school, take the time to ask them how they want to participate. This is a critical step in diminishing adult control and empowering the students. For example, schedule a "working lunch" where you get together with a group of students to discuss how they want to be empowered in the school community. Since you can't have lunch with every student in a reasonable amount of time, send out a Google Survey or create a suggestion box in the office and have kids share their ideas for how they see their role in the school.

- **Play that funky music.** Instead of trying to micromanage the most unstructured time of the day, give the children some parameters and lots of choice. Make the lunch and recess experience all about the kids—let them socialize. Give them choices about where and with whom they want to sit, and let the music play. Cantiague has introduced a DJ of the Week program. Each week a child or group of children picks an artist they want to spotlight and they play that artist's music during the lunch period. Have you ever seen how most children react to music? They love it and it creates a unifying experience. Stop trying to keep the lunchroom quiet and orderly—let the kids have some (safe) fun and play that funky music!

- **Exercise student voice.** What gets reinforced and celebrated becomes the norm and is embedded in the school's culture. Knowing that children contribute ideas that will be acted on has a huge impact on the way kids feel toward the school experience. Let kids make the morning announcements or give them a chance to be "student ambassadors" who provide tours to new families, serve as buddies to new students, and offer information to visitors. Focus on the single goal to spotlight and celebrate kids. For example, Cantiague uses positive behavior referral forms where a staff member or student can describe something positive a student has done and submit it to Tony. He then calls the parent to share the positive note and within a few days, the note is read aloud to the entire school and the child is recognized as a "Bucket Filler of the Week" who has done something positive for him/herself or others.

- **Give kids choices within the curriculum.** Let's give teachers the space to make every activity in the classroom more student-centered by giving kids some choice in what they learn and how they share their understandings. Instead of standardizing every assignment so every child is doing the same thing at the same time, teachers should feel free to try changing things up. Yes, as leaders we may want to ensure that every fifth grader writes a research essay as part of the writing workshop experience, but we need to empower our teachers so they know they have the ability to personalize the learning experience for their students. For example, we should support teachers when they want to let the children choose research topics they are passionate about instead of assigning them the topic during the essay writing unit. The standards and skills will still be addressed when teachers are empowered to share control of the learning with the children.

A BLUEPRINT FOR FULL IMPLEMENTATION

Step 1: Create a shared decision-making team.

Shared decision-making embraces the equal participation of teachers, support staff, families, students, and administration as they collaborate to discuss school-related issues. Including students on the team allows them ownership. The intention is not merely to acknowledge their right to express opinions, but to truly hear them, acting on their ideas and suggestions, and addressing their passions. Integrating students fully into the team as active participants is critical. Children need to see their ideas come to fruition so they develop a sense of agency. The whole team, but especially the students, should share the conviction that students are valued and respected members of the school community.

Step 2: Encourage student participation on committees.

Rather than giving lip service to student involvement by giving one student delegate a nominal position on school-wide committees as the student representative, give the children a real voice by offering students multiple opportunities for genuine participation. For example, it is imperative that we start including students in the hiring of new staff. Yes, teachers and parents should play a role in this process too, but kids are the ones who will have the most interaction with new staff members. Although they may not be looking for the same qualities or talking points that adults attend to, they have keen insight into who they feel comfortable around and strong opinions about their feelings. If you're not ready for kids to join this process, have them participate in the health and safety committee where they could have input on everything from the food served in the lunchroom to the safety procedures in place throughout the building.

Step 3: Create a Brilliance Builder lab.

Children can drive the learning and share their knowledge using a variety of media with Brilliance Builder, which blends together the notions of Genius Hour and Makerspace. This is an opportunity to flip the learning so children as young as kindergarteners pursue the ideas, topics, or concepts that are of interest to them. They are given a space to create, make, tinker, or build in a way that is meaningful to them.

Whether they are making with LEGOs, creating with Tinkertoys, or building circuits, children are accessing their genius to innovate. Rather than having adults control student activities through the whole day, students have the opportunity to lead their own learning, with the adults serving as guides or assistants when necessary. The adults are there to support students as they become experts in an area of their choice. The children then share their Brilliance Builder creations, projects, or activities with the world—publicizing their work gives students a chance to be a lead learner by unleashing their brilliance to a huge audience.

Step 4: Initiate a student EdCamp.

Set up the school day using the EdCamp model so children have choice in their learning each day. Glenn Robbins models student EdCamp in his New Jersey middle school by building in time for students to facilitate their own EdCamp, organizing the day and leading their own learning. Children have expertise and incredibly developed skillsets, so let them share and learn with each other.

OVERCOMING PUSHBACK

Let's be honest. Many educators are control freaks, so relinquishing control over decisions they've been used to making is going to be really, really tough. When schools operate the way they have always functioned—adults controlling students, emphasizing curriculum coverage, breeding compliance and obedience—less effort is required. Any plan to change an existing system to create schools that work better for kids will lead to some amount of pushback.

Our teachers are just not ready to give students that much input into daily instruction. Fine—teachers learn and grow at their own rates. Maybe they can start at the other end with assessment. Subtle changes in the way we assess students can give them a voice in the learning process. For example, after every learning experience students can self-assess and reflect on how they engaged in the learning. Reflection and self-assessment help students understand themselves as learners and encourage them to internalize their learning.

If self-assessment seems like something teachers want to try later on, they can give the students choices in how they express their knowledge. If they are doing a unit on a historical period, every student does not need to sit through a test at the end of the unit to communicate understanding—give them choices. Let them recreate a village using LEGOs or Minecraft; challenge them to keep a diary as if they were living during that time; let them write and perform a play highlighting certain aspects of the culture. Some teachers create choice boards for students, which allow them to choose how they are going to express their knowledge and understanding during a specific learning experience.

These kids are too young to make good decisions. How can I expect a five-year-old to tell me what he wants to learn when he can't even tie his shoelaces? How can a fifth-grader offer us valuable input during the hiring process for a new teacher when all she wants to do is have fun all day? How can we trust a high school student to facilitate our school-wide Twitter account when he barely makes it to class on time? Comments like these show valid concerns about relinquishing control and empowering students; there may be some truth to the idea that students need to understand the ramifications of their decisions when they have others depending on them. Although we could give in to this concern, we must help reframe the "problem" and start to see developing student agency as an opportunity.

Again, start with baby steps by giving students voice in ways that will help them understand that their ideas matter. For example, ask the children about the food served in the lunchroom and find out what they like and why they like it. Survey the children about the recess experience—do they prefer it to be more structured in nature or more open-ended? Their answers may surprise you. Take the time to speak with students and help them find their voices and develop agency because those are the skills that will make kids career and life ready. Once they have proven their capacity to make good decisions in matters that concern them alone, they will be ready to take on bigger challenges.

Teachers are not going to be able to teach all of their content if they let students take control. Teachers are used to planning for every moment of the day to ensure that they are effectively covering the curriculum and implementing successful classroom management techniques. Let's start by relieving teachers of that constant pressure to cover the content. Shift the focus to teaching students and meeting their needs. We will certainly hold to a set of acceptable standards to ensure that children are being exposed to essential skills and subject matter, but how they learn and what resources they use can be decided collaboratively between teachers and students. Start small: Offer students input into one subject or unit. Once everyone feels comfortable with the change, go from there.

Offering children time each week to research self-selected topics not only motivates them to invest in their own learning, but develops their literacy skills and forges connections between content areas.

Encourage teachers to plan together to create interdisciplinary projects that address multiple topics and content areas while also immersing the children in learning experiences over an extended period of time. When this plan has been established, share it with the children in the form of an essential question that will guide the unit and give the children an opportunity to explore beyond what has been pre-planned by the teachers.

Eliminate any tests and let the children show you what they know in ways that matter to them so that assessment becomes part of the journey and not the end of it. This is a subtle and easy way to amplify student voice and give them some ownership over the learning.

If you are ready to throw everything out, including the standardized curriculum, and make the whole day an ongoing learning experience directed by the children, then go for it. Extend the Brilliance Builder model beyond its typical forty-minute period per week and found all your learning experiences in its philosophy. Let every period have a little Genius Hour in it; let every learning experience include some type of Makerspace activity so they become the norm and not the exception.

THE HACK IN ACTION

Cantiague has two fifth-grade representatives on its shared decision-making team, which is comprised of the students, four parents, four teachers, two teacher aides, and the administrators. The children on this team have equal voice. They often lead initiatives that are important to them and consistently offer relevant and valuable agenda items. Over the past two years, the student representatives helped implement the DJ of the Week program, where music featuring a different classical, jazz, rock, or pop musician gets played in the lunchroom once a week. Last year they helped revamp Field Day so it is more consistent with a Color War that some students had experienced at sleep away camps, and the feedback was incredibly positive.

If you aren't ready to assign students seats at the conference table, then let them address a topic that is of the highest importance to them: homework. Since homework isn't likely to be eliminated any time soon, why not try rebranding it and make it something kids can get excited about each night? For example, give learners choices by creating a menu of activities to extend their learning. Instead of having seventh-graders read about the Civil War in a textbook and answer the questions at the end of the chapter, give them a choice to create a video about what could have happened if the South had won the war, or start a blog in the persona of a Yankee soldier, or create a historical fiction picture book based on the war.

If you are ready to take the homework hack a step further, have the children engage in Brilliance Builder or Genius Hour activities at home, where they create something from scratch or pursue a passion. You can start by incorporating "Try It Tuesday," where the "homework" every Tuesday night is to try a new activity, such as creating an artwork in a new medium, engaging in a maker activity, researching a passion, conducting a science experiment, or anything else that interests them. The students can share their experiences the next day in school. Trying new things seems like the perfect way to extend the learning beyond the school day and personalize it so each child explores a topic he or she wants to learn about. Implementing low-stakes activities like this slowly shifts a school so it works for kids.

Once students and teachers have experience with such less threatening adjustments, consider ways to make the learning that unfolds during the school day more student-centered and student-driven. Although many schools are experimenting with Genius Hour or Makerspace, or both, we hear that it can sometimes be a challenge to find the time to fit them into the school day. With ease of implementation and execution in mind, please consider the Brilliance Builder option. It incorporates the best features of both models: the creativity, the making, and the genius-driven learning. Brilliance Builder allows children to drive the learning based on their passions, interests, and expertise. The builder aspect of this movement encourages students to create or make something related to research they conduct into their passion, bridging Genius Hour and Makerspace movements.

Offering children time each week to research self-selected topics not only motivates them to invest in their own learning, but develops their literacy skills and forges connections between content areas.

Brilliance Builder enhances students' 21st century skill set with particular emphasis on critical thinking, creating, and communicating their understandings.

We know from our experience that educators make thousands of decisions every day that are in their students' best interests. For the most part these decisions are successful, and we work hard to give our students what they need. Even though we're already doing so many things right, we cannot forget the importance of taking student voices into account, especially when decisions have a direct impact on them and their learning.

Our students have important insights and valuable perspectives, and from our vantage point they are our most important stakeholders, so listening to our kids and acting on their ideas should be a priority. We may have to get comfortable with relinquishing some of the control, but amplifying student voice and empowering students to have a say in the future of their school and their learning will ensure that our schools work for kids.

HACK 7

HIRE SUPERSTARS
Develop a team of exceptional educators

*A good teacher is like a candle—it consumes
itself to light the way for others.*
— MUSTAFA KEMAL ATATÜRK, FIRST PRESIDENT OF TURKEY

THE PROBLEM: THE TEACHER SHORTAGE IS REAL

THE US DEPARTMENT of Education Statistics reports that nearly 17% of teachers leave the classroom in their first five years (2015). Enrollment in teacher preparation programs in California is down 53% over the last five years. Fewer teachers are leaving college prepared, finding an initial position where they can grow into the profession, or staying in the education system. The reasons for these trends are complicated, but negative cultural attitudes toward educators certainly contribute to the dynamic. No education system will prosper without renewing itself with excellent educators. Recruiting the best teachers and retaining them so they can become mentors is one of the best things leaders can do for students across the country.

THE HACK: HIRE SUPERSTARS

America is simply infatuated with fame. We're enthralled by people we have never met who entertain us from places that we will probably never go. We cheer passionately for people we see on a field for a few hours a week. We listen to stories about celebrities and daydream about what it must be like to live such a pampered life. Our kids hero-worship athletes, actors, and musicians, often without recognizing the hard work and sacrifice that success requires. Those people who perform on stage, screen, and field represent a minute percentage of the population that has been gifted with extraordinary talent. They are exceptional at their jobs, and we marvel at their abilities. When a public figure steps to the podium after a game or features in a talk show, we want to listen. We hang on every word of a movie and sit on the edge of our chairs during a game.

Teachers don't experience that kind of focused esteem even though they work extremely hard and many are talented beyond words. Teachers guide a disparate group of kids through the perils of the 180-day school year, motivating reluctant and unprepared followers to take risky leaps from one level of understanding and ability to the next. They make connections with kids, some of whom have not yet acquired the social skills to forge healthy relationships. They create nurturing environments that put students at the center of the learning. They take stacks of work home every night, every weekend, every holiday, sacrificing family time to help children who may not want or appreciate their help. Their accomplishments rarely get acknowledged, much less celebrated, and yet teachers carry on this relentless pace through careers that last for thirty years or more. There is something deeply hypocritical about a society that claims to value education highly while devoting excessive time, money, and reverence to entertainment. If we truly care about education, we need to emphasize the role our teachers play and fill our schools with only the very best educators.

Your legacy for your school can be a team of exceptional educators. Create this team of superstars by hacking the hiring practices so that new teachers coming into your system already exhibit stellar qualities.

WHAT YOU CAN DO TOMORROW

- **Start a Google Doc with job descriptions.** Create a document with all of the current job descriptions in your organization. This gives you a starting point and develops a transparency in the process.

- **Generate buzz about job openings.** Post the job openings in high-traffic areas where they will be noticed. Now that you have active social media platforms, use those as well. Appeal to possible candidates by celebrating the great things going on in your school: "Are you ready to join a group of innovative educators?"

- **Connect with local universities.** Offer to present a topic to students in their pre-service classes. This will give you an opportunity to promote your school and make connections with potential candidates

A BLUEPRINT FOR FULL IMPLEMENTATION

Step 1: Collaborate to create job descriptions.

The best people to know what a staff position entails are those who are already doing it. Ask a team of grade- or subject-level teachers to create the job description for any position that is coming open. Pay them to do it—developing job descriptions is outside their regular duties. Most teachers who are committed to the school community would do it for free, but that's not the point. Don't let a few hundred dollars get in the way of this perfect opportunity to set expectations with staff input.

The leader in the building could clearly come up with a description of the position. However, taking teacher voices into account waylays objections that the leader is too distanced from the classroom to know what really happens there. A teacher's ground-level perspective may offer insight into what sort of candidate would be a good fit for a particular situation. The other benefit of having staff create the job description is that they develop agreement on what meets essential criteria for the job. If one of them is not meeting those expectations herself, it will be much easier for you to have the conversation about how things could and should be going.

When the document is completed, sit down with the creators and talk about the components of the job description so they can reflect about the relevance of these components to their own work. Ask questions about how they are being supported in those areas and what they need to move themselves forward. Such a dialogue shows that you value their needs and desires.

Step 2: Start with a conversation.

We may recognize truth in the cliché "Don't judge a book by its cover," but when we interview teachers we rarely get past the cover letter and resumé. Certainly, candidates whose accomplishments distinguish them get interviews, but many potential superstar teachers get overlooked due to lack of experience. Conversely, some people get interviews based on their ability to write a cover letter, which does not necessarily correlate with how they relate to kids. Once our paper screening is completed, we do background checks on all of the candidates we feel should receive a quick interview with the administrator. Getting beyond the curriculum vitae means having real conversations with candidates. Set up screener interviews with three times the number of candidates you want as finalists. So, if you want to add five members to the team, you should screen fifteen candidates. Our screener interviews are twenty minutes long. We don't ask any more than three questions during that time, but usually the best candidates use these questions as a springboard to initiate meaningful conversation.

Step 3: Ask fewer questions, conduct more conversation.

Avoid interview questions that have a canned correct answer. Using situational questions gives the candidate a chance to demonstrate flexible and judicious thinking. Make sure all of your stakeholder groups are represented on the team. You'll have done the groundwork to ensure that you have confidence in everyone attending the final interviews. Having staff, board members, parents, and students on the team can be very beneficial to the process. We don't play "gotcha" during the interview process. This is not a time to decide whether or not the person can think on their feet in front of ten people. We have the questions available for the candidates when they arrive. You could also choose to give the questions to the candidates before they arrive. We want their best work. Giving them every opportunity to succeed is important.

Step 4: Conduct student-led tours.

You have seen their paper resumés and cover letters, conducted background checks, and had a twenty-minute screener interview with them. Invite the stand-out individual candidates to your school for student-guided tours. Let the candidates know that this is part of the interview process: We want to be transparent, but we also want to get firsthand knowledge from the students in how the candidate interacts with them throughout the tour. Elementary, middle, and high school students can all be trusted to walk candidates through the building and show them features of the building and the learning taking place.

Step 5: Set up a site visit.

Taking a trip to see how the candidate interacts with kids in the classroom is a fantastic way to come to a final decision. It is not always an easy thing to do for a couple of reasons. The candidate may be from a different state and that could clearly be a travel issue. The opportunity to set up something virtually may allow you to see what the classroom looks like and also to test the teacher's technological knowledge, if that is an important component of what your team needs. We will only do site visits with finalists and only if they are comfortable with us being in that space. We don't want to cause an issue, but we also want to see people in their element if the final candidates are close. If this is not an option, teaching or leading a group on your site could work.

Step 6: Integrate the new staff member.

There will be plenty of time to show the new staff member how to negotiate the building and where to find supplies. You only have one chance to ensure the newcomer feels excited to belong to your crew. Here is an opportunity to prove your commitment to putting people first in school culture. New staff members will benefit from any of the following:

- Get them involved in curriculum work right away;
- Facilitate team connections over the summer;
- Invite them to summer social events;
- Incorporate three days of optional learning before the school year starts: technology integration day, mentor day, goal-setting day;
- Give them time to hang out with mentors so they can meet early, go out to lunch, or simply chill in the classroom.

Step 7: Create a "press conference" to announce new team members.

Give them a bunch of new school gear, let them step up to the podium, and record the event for your school community to watch later. This is a great way for your district to introduce new people, and one of our favorite things to do. Set up a staging area that has a district logo behind the candidate. Provide a script you would see when a professional athletic team introduces a new player to the media. Make a big deal about your new "draft pick" and how this superstar is going to help your organization move forward. Give the new hire a chance to say a few words and end the press conference by giving the new staff member some district attire to hold up for pictures. Take it to a new level by adding kids to the audience so they can interact with the new teacher.

Step 8: Facilitate mentoring.

Having a mentor keeps new teachers headed in the right direction. Since your veteran teachers helped create job descriptions, they will have insight into expectations and a common language with the new teacher when they collaborate. Make time for them to connect on a regular basis. Coach the mentors as well as the mentees so they have the right tools to increase the capacity of the new hire.

Step 9: Invest time.

Follow through on your intention to check on new staff members throughout the year. Schedule it. Find time. Make time. There's a good chance that they'll be part of the school for twenty years or more, so you'll want them to have a strong start. The first years are a time of exponential growth and uncertainty for new teachers; for them to work at optimal levels they need to feel valued. If you've chosen a good candidate, this teacher will be instrumental in your culture of innovation and exceptional learning. You help shape the culture by investing time in people.

Step 10: Revisit job descriptions annually.

Allow staff to make changes in the way positions are defined. Making this activity a priority and designating a time for it each year shows you value the staff's time and opinions.

OVERCOMING PUSHBACK

How can we come to consensus on job descriptions? We have worked in school districts that have three first-grade teachers and we have worked in others that have sixty. The process has to adapt to the environment, but a few tenets can remain consistent. The collective voice is clearly better, but having sixty people in a room trying to create a document is not a great use of everyone's time. Here are a few things that can honor voice, even if everyone is not in the room:

- Ask all staff members in a grade level or department a few essential questions through a survey tool. Some possible questions are:

    What do you value most about your job?
    What is the best part of your day in your job?
    What three skills are most important for students to attain in your grade level or department?

- Once you have input on essential values and skills from the department, develop a smaller team to take on the task of identifying the larger group's key skills and values.

- Create a Google Doc for the team to collaborate. Understand that the most important thing about a job description is that people need to be able to own it and live it; otherwise, it turns into another piece of paper that is put in a binder on a shelf. The length of the description will have a direct impact on whether people will remember it. Use simple language and make straightforward points about the skills and values your department or grade level holds as non-negotiable.

- Prior to bringing the description to the entire department make sure all skills and values identified in the original survey have been addressed.

- Don't be afraid to roll it out with fanfare. People should be able to celebrate the job description. Come up with something visible to celebrate a collaborative process.

Won't teachers want to make the job descriptions less work-intensive than they should be? Most teachers are proud of the work they do and recognize its importance, so this is unlikely, but we know that giving someone the keys to the car doesn't make him a good driver. Allowing staff members to create their own job descriptions could set you up for a watered-down version of what that job should look like, but if you have invested the time it takes to be an outstanding leader, you already know where trouble spots may be in the school and can make that process more collaborative in nature. It is a great opportunity for a dialogue on what the job should or could look like. Having a process in place that values staff opinions can spark those conversations and help everyone know they are in it together.

The promise doesn't match the experience. Trust the process that you have put in place, but understand that we all miss the mark from time to time. You are trying to implement a way to attract and retain the best possible people for students in your school. Sometimes the fit just isn't right for the new person or the team. We try to hire people we aspire to be like, not those who will keep us in status quo, but there are scenarios where things just don't work out. It is better to help that person move on to a better situation than to leave someone in a spot where you know she won't be effective.

THE HACK IN ACTION

One essential piece to hacking the hiring process is student involvement. If we are going to create spaces that are about students, we have to offer authentic opportunities for students to be invested in the process. Recently Fall Creek hired a high school principal. We knew student voice needed to be at the forefront of the hire so we asked the staff for suggestions about students who could serve as active members of the team. We weren't looking for the star athlete or the class president. We wanted kids who excelled, but we also wanted those who struggled. We wanted a cross section of the school, not only the kids who are on every committee. Our student group consisted of musicians, athletes, honor roll students, and those who struggled academically.

The process started with a conversation between our administrative team and the students. We wanted the kids to express what they wanted in a building leader. We asked them for potential interview questions that we could bring to the team, and had them describe what they would like their involvement to look like throughout the process. We knew going in that we would say yes to essentially any role they wanted to play, but finding out where they wanted to be involved was an incredible experience for the administrators. The students expressed interest in being on one of the hiring teams, directing tours of the building for the candidates, and then debriefing with the full committee when they convened after all of the interviews were completed. They also wanted to meet with the superintendent after the process. The conviction in their voices and enthusiasm for being active members of the team was jaw-dropping.

Throughout their involvement they did not shy away from any

conversation. They brought their opinions to the group in a room full of their teachers, parents, and administrators. They talked about their tours and how the candidates interacted with other students and teachers. They reflected and spoke eloquently about the type of leader they wanted to follow. They were spectacular.

When we came up with a finalist, we made sure the students knew about the recommendation for hire at the same time as the hiring team, as they were clearly valued members of that committee. Roughly a week after the process was complete Joe received a call from one of the teachers who had been a member of the interview team. He was glowing in his praise for the process. Not only did he appreciate being part of the team, he could not stop talking about the impact the process had on the students. The kids on the interview team walked through the hallways with new-found confidence. They were empowered. They were part of a culture change. They were leaders. They just didn't know it until they had a chance to lead.

Hiring excellent staff is one of the most important things we can do for students. We want the right group of people in front of kids, people who share a positive, innovative mindset. Look for a candidate's potential rather than ability to teach a particular grade. Acquiring a constant learner who develops incredible relationships with kids should be at the forefront of the interview process: It's easier to teach the right person how to work at a different grade level than it is to find those exceptional candidates. Do everything you can to make successful applicants feel welcome so they can begin contributing actively to your community. That process starts from the minute they walk in the room during a screening interview and continues to the press conference that announces them to the world. Celebrate your new teachers' strengths and abilities and nurture them so they help your school to flourish.

PASSION PROJECTS FOR ADULTS
Empower teachers to control their own learning

Don't aim for success if you want it. Just do what
you love and believe in and it will come naturally.
—SIR DAVID FROST, TELEVISION HOST

THE PROBLEM: STAFF MEMBERS NEED TIME TO CULTIVATE PROFESSIONAL GROWTH

ASTOUNDINGLY, SUPERVISORS ASK teachers to differentiate instruction for each student even as they continue to give exactly the same professional development to every instructor. Administrators often put teachers from assorted grade levels, content areas, knowledge bases, and interest ranges in a room for full-day training, expecting the quality of education teachers offer to improve as a result. While there are clearly times that all educators in a building need the same information, each teacher needs individualized learning as well. If differentiation meets the individual needs of all learners, then this best practice should apply to the professionals as well as to their students.

We know you may not have control over district, state, or federal initiatives. Until educators have a strong voice in such organizations, having initiatives imposed on us is our reality. If you're asked to be part of the decision-making body, go do it. If no one approaches you, seek out opportunities to participate in influential groups. Hacking leadership is about finding a way to succeed by circumventing obstacles. As we deal with the system as it now exists, we can hack ways to meet the individual needs of staff members while still maintaining the integrity of initiatives.

THE HACK: PASSION PROJECTS FOR ADULTS

Our students have profited extensively from Genius Hour, a specific time for them to learn about something that interests them and to express that learning in any format that they choose. It occurred to us that we could pattern professional development on this success, creating opportunities for teachers to learn what they want, when they want, and how they want. While scheduling a specific hour for students to explore their passions integrates well with the current model of the school day, reserving similar time for teacher learning presents problems.

Aside from the issue of what to do with the students while their teachers are learning, holding any school time sacrosanct for a particular purpose is almost impossible for teachers, considering the variables that affect every workday. Teachers have a propensity to "eat last," or not at all, when it comes to their learning, often because a teacher's job involves such a variety of complex tasks that little time is left over for lunch, let alone learning. Professionals deserve our trust in their desire to improve and extend their learning. Passion projects allow individual staff members to delve into topics they feel passionately about exploring while administrative teams provide the time, resources, and opportunities for the learning to flourish.

The passion project professional growth model allows people to choose topics and decide on a personalized learning plan. We have not rejected any teacher's learning plan goal in the last three years. We want people to own the process and take it on in a way that suits them. We trust teachers to find an effective process, although we specify two non-negotiable elements:

1) Every plan must include a student data component so teachers can reflect on the process and satisfy state requirements for educator/teacher effectiveness or whatever your state is calling it. Analyzing student data allows educators to reflect on ways to integrate emerging trends and patterns into practical classroom applications. We want to be very clear that the data should *inform* but not *drive* decision-making. There is a distinct difference. When data informs decisions, teaching professionals consider the data and other relevant information to find ways to improve student learning. In contrast, having data drive decisions implies that reading the data objectively determines future actions. Many factors should influence decisions about instruction, and we want to give the professionals who work with the students on a regular basis the latitude to make decisions as they see fit.

2) We ask simply that teachers strive to get better. As teachers work to improve, leaders must be willing to stand back and allow them to progress at their own paces. Growth is particular to each individual—teachers change at different rates according to their needs, backgrounds, and abilities. We have to trust people to improve without constantly trying to quantify that improvement. We want to make sure we are not criticizing someone's growth, especially since making errors is a common sign of taking risks. Progressing in a complicated endeavor like teaching tends to be a recursive process, one that is unlikely to happen if teachers do not feel wholly committed to their goals. Trust your staff to be professional by allowing them to take ownership of their own learning.

We have seen a significant increase in collaborative effort as teachers work through their growth model goals. Most goals are more carefully written, more rigorous, and more innovative than they were before we initiated passion projects. People take bigger risks when they set their own goals because they feel personally compelled to increase their capacity to help students. Even though a few teachers will try to skirt the system by creating a goal that is easily attainable, remember that allowing teachers to choose their own goals has not caused these people to "cop out." They would have done the same thing with the antiquated processes of the past. Rather than responding to the problematic few by attempting to control everyone, we need to make decisions based on our best people. They are the ones we need to make happy. Giving teachers the opportunity to own their learning from start to finish shows how much we value their work and abilities.

WHAT YOU CAN DO TOMORROW

Stepping out of the professional development comfort zone is going to take some time and a great deal of trust. When you implement passion projects some staff members may search desperately for a topic they can commit to. Many have been told how, when, and what they will learn for years. What you can do tomorrow is provide time, resources, and opportunities for your staff to engage in professional growth. Finding ways to offer any of these three things to your staff right away will establish innovation and ownership as part of school culture. Once staff members trust the process, they'll be eager to continue learning on their own.

- **Get teachers thinking about their passions.** Introduce the idea of passion projects and ask teachers to begin thinking about what they want to work on so that they will be prepared to dive into their projects as soon as you can make time available to them.

- **Pass good resources on to teachers.** Once you know the goals and interests of your staff members you may be able to provide suggestions for relevant resources. This is where we see leaders moving to the middle to facilitate the passion projects. We are not leading the charge, but connecting staff members and resources. Find connections between different topics of interest so you can put people into contact with each other. Keep your staff in mind when you come upon resources, whether online, face-to-face, or in books and journals. Shoot off a short email or stick a photocopy in a teacher's mailbox. Both of us use Twitter a great deal, so when we see an article or resource on Twitter that would fit someone's goals, we retweet the post and tag the staff member. Giving specific help with resources need not cut into the budget and it's worth your effort because supporting professional growth is such an essential component to growing as a staff. Proving that you value a teacher's work elevates your instructional leadership.

- **Provide opportunities for informal meetings.** The first step is to listen when you ask your staff what kinds of connections they need. Then, find a way to make opportunities for those connections to happen. This could be in an "Appy Hour" after school where staff connect and talk about apps that are working in their classrooms. It could be in a "Lunch and Learn" where a group spends time discussing a topic of their choice. It could be an asynchronous meeting using a platform like Voxer to discuss a book or topic of their choice. Understand that the opportunity to connect may yield few results when you start. Your first meeting may attract only three people, but think of it this way: Three people showed up and learned something. Once word gets around that the meeting was useful, more people will filter in.

A BLUEPRINT FOR FULL IMPLEMENTATION

Step 1: Identify the goals that your district deems essential.

Identifying goals gives the group a compass as they navigate the work to be done. Even if the work is mandated, try to find aspects of the goals that are personally meaningful. Each group member can decide how his or her own goals for growth connect to the district approach. Imposed mandates should not drive their processes but inform them.

Step 2: Ask staff for input.

Ask staff members to identify which personal or professional matters they would like to improve. The only caveat is that their work can't cost the district any money in resources. This discussion will empower your teachers. Ask why they want to get better at a certain practice—they already know. They'll break down their own teaching skills without any need to have awkward one-on-one conversations about what they need to improve. Showing confidence in a teacher's desire and ability to progress develops mutual trust.

Step 3: Integrate student data components into the goals.

We need to include some sort of measurable data points to adhere to the district or state goals. By discussing where they want to improve first, you already have teachers thinking about how they could fold what they want to learn into the initiative. Adding the data component will make these more personal goals work for a district, state, or federal system. It also helps to eliminate the complaint that mandates continually add just "one more thing" to teachers' jobs. If we can use their passion to improve instruction and connect it to a data component that satisfies a state requirement, we are helping them clear something from a plate that is already full.

Step 4: Ask teachers to find a mentor.

Teachers should identify mentors who will help them learn more than they might learn alone. They don't need to tell you who the mentor is, but everyone needs to connect with someone who has expertise in the area of inquiry. As a leader, your conversations about passion projects will give you the information you need to help teachers connect with a mentor. Forging connections between mentors and mentees will bolster everyone's professional growth.

Step 5: Give teachers unstructured time to work on professional development.

Destroy the PD schedule and inspire teachers to work on passion projects. Having limited school time has been a continual problem that obstructs new endeavors—after all, teachers spend the vast majority of their days interacting with children and the rest of it planning and grading. Administrators have traditionally addressed the restricted time available for professional development by structuring that time rigorously.

When we overschedule we run the risk of hindering the growth of our best teachers, most of whom would gleefully take an opportunity to be unscheduled for a day to work on their own development because they have been squeezing it into their own evenings and weekends. Teachers who are not committed to their growth are going to grade papers, plan lessons, or answer emails regardless of your schedule—they'll bring that work right into the meeting room. The best teachers are going to engage on their own level, which is much closer to the level you'd wish them to attain than you may realize. If we trust teachers to use the time to get better, they will.

Take the next professional development day and say, "Today, there is no agenda—you're going to work on your own professional goals. Wait…one agenda item…we are going to have lunch together from 11:30-1:00. We're going to sit, eat, and talk about things that have nothing to do with school." Guess what is going to happen: They are going to work and talk about school and it is going to be incredibly meaningful.

> **Passion projects empowered people to reach beyond what they thought possible in their learning.**

Allowing them to work on their own agenda and goals will convince far more teachers to engage in professional development than you probably thought possible. The look on our teachers' faces when we told them there were three designated PD days throughout the year with *no agenda* was priceless. The feedback after those days was even better. Our groups got much more completed when we scheduled less. Trust your educators to spend time thinking about their goals. Reflection is a tremendous key to growth and overscheduling definitely gets in the way of the reflection process.

Step 6: Be flexible.

We ask all staff members to reflect on the project in any way they see fit. We have a reflection template that they certainly can use, but we encourage people to find new ways to demonstrate their learning. Not only does this expand their knowledge, it gives them another medium to use in their classrooms. We have received videos, podcasts, live binders, websites, and formal "pitch presentations" as evidence for growth over the course of the year. Allow staff to be creative and be flexible in how they demonstrate their learning.

Step 7: Provide quality feedback.

Providing quality feedback on the passion projects ensures that teachers know their voices have been heard and their work is valued. Lead learners model the type of specific feedback that should be happening in classrooms by taking the time to think carefully about what teachers need to hear. This process will take time, but the payoff is incredible. Being specific is key. We use the phrases "I like..." and "I wonder..." as a structure for feedback. Recently we have found that using voice notes to give feedback for goals makes the process easier. The staff reaction to this has been fantastic. They really enjoyed hearing genuine excitement in our tones as we discussed their ideas.

OVERCOMING PUSHBACK

How am I supposed to convince the whole staff this change is necessary? If your reality is that you need to implement a new initiative, then leverage the opinion leaders on your staff to drive it. Opinion leaders, those with social influence and specific content knowledge, are crucial to the success of a new initiative like passion projects because they guide those who tend to be followers. When opinion leaders get interested in an initiative, they lead the social system in the direction of their interests. Others will be influenced by their knowledge and skillset, and you'll not need to engage in a battle of wills with naysayers.

How can I convince staff to engage? Consider what type of social system your teachers form. Opinion leaders are more influential in a heterophilous social system (one with diverse members) because their actions will influence the non-elite members. This type of system generates new ideas because it involves more interaction from different backgrounds, often initiating change as a result. Innovators in a homophilous system (one with similar values and beliefs) are regarded as suspiciously "different," so change needs to happen on a broader scale before it feels safe. The personal charisma of the opinion leader in this type of social system tends to be the key to whether or not the group accepts or rejects an innovation. Once you understand the social system you're dealing with, you can use a systematic approach to sustain progress over time.

Some teachers are just going to waste the time instead of learning. The simple answer is those teachers were going to grade or surf the Internet or waste time some other way, so why would we hold our great people back on account of those few? If we make decisions based on our best people, we'll choose to offer autonomy. Teachers will be held accountable for their time when they provide evidence of growth at the end of the year.

THE HACK IN ACTION

When Joe began his job as superintendent in Fall Creek he brought together representatives from the elementary, middle, and high schools in the district to talk about professional development. When the focus group assembled he asked them two questions. The first was, "Are you a better teacher than when you arrived in Fall Creek?" All members of the group nodded their heads or blurted out "Yes" even before the question was finished. The second question was, "How do you know?" The reaction to this question was much different. Everyone looked around, paused, started to talk, paused a little more, and the answer was evident in the silence. Every person at that table might have become a better teacher during his or her time in the district, but no one knew for sure. The aims that group developed were simple: Help teachers get better, and make sure people know how they have grown since their first day with the district.

When the group had this discussion, Genius Hour, 20% time, or Google time projects were influencing the educational world. Students in multiple classrooms, including those in the Fall Creek district, were following their passions for a portion of the day. The focus group thought that taking the same approach to professional development would capitalize on a tremendous amount of momentum that was already moving the students forward. Teachers marveled at how students were engaging in the process and taking ownership of that time, and we asked, "What if staff felt the same way?"

This is where Fall Creek's passion projects originated. A spectacular growth surge happened over the course of the next three years. Conversations in hallways and classrooms focused less on initiatives and more on growth. Teachers talked about comfort zones and how to get out of their own. They embraced their own learning. The district provided time, resources, and opportunity to connect for those who were using the process. Passion projects empowered people to reach beyond what they thought possible in their learning.

Most important, the culture shifted. The teachers' experiences of owning their learning influenced classroom dynamics beyond the designated project time. Moving to individualized, learner-centered professional development proved to be transformational. The change was not a mandate, and the district staff still met every requirement set forth by the state. The process wasn't more work; it was the right work done more. In 2016, the International Center for Leadership in Education named the Fall Creek School District an Innovative District due to its incorporation of passion projects.

When we commit to a project and feel ownership of it, we feel pride in its impact. Passion projects are a source of pride for their creators, but more important, they have a definite impact. The benefits of passion projects' self-directed, individualized learning transfers from teachers to their students. We want teachers to be thinkers. We want them to be problem-solvers because we *need* them to instill those attributes in their students.

We make an error when we treat professional development as if it is divorced from real practice. In our urgency to improve everything we can, too many initiatives and mandates get imposed, and consequently people have little to no ownership, which has led to disengagement. Though we may not be able to control what happens at the state and national levels, we have found a way to value the voice of our staffs by listening and allowing them to drive their learning. We want that for our kids and we need to model it with our instructional leaders. We hired professionals—let's treat them professionally.

This passion project approach serves as the impetus for our take on professional development in the form of collective learning experiences. Both aspects of professional development are essential to developing a well-informed, passionate, and cohesive staff.

COLLABORATE AND LEARN
Facilitate collective professional development

*If you want to be a master teacher, you
must be a master learner.*
—George Couros, Educator and Innovator

THE PROBLEM: EDUCATORS RARELY GET TO
LEARN TOGETHER AND FROM EACH OTHER

INSTEAD OF STARTING with the perceived needs of the organization to plan for learning, we have suggested pursuing individual interests as a way to enhance and refine teachers' skills. The next step in hacking professional development is bringing those individuals together to learn and develop a collective vision and goals for the organization by building on individual passions and expertise. This collaborative learning approach to professional development will create a sustainable organization while also resonating with individuals on a personal level.

Participating in learning activities designed to educate, nurture, and support us should be a professional responsibility that happens collectively. It should also feel joyful and valuable. Often, though, it doesn't feel like that at all. Thomas Guskey offers a hint about why so many educators dread PD days when he notes that good professional development is intentional, ongoing, and systemic in nature. Juxtapose Guskey's list with what usually happens, and teachers' criticism of professional development seems justified. We would argue that many educators feel they are being exposed to low-quality professional development that seems irrelevant and disjointed, as if it was planned in a silo by a disconnected administrator. Because it was.

Professional development for educators has become a special event that happens periodically throughout the year in a decontextualized and unsustainable way. We have all been there: sitting for hours in isolation while someone lectures us about all the things we are supposed to be doing, couching it as meaningful learning. The type of professional development where a presenter talks at a group of educators has come to be known as "sit and get."

> If educators feel passionately about an idea and see value in it, the chances of their using it as a focal point for future learning—both individually and collectively—increases exponentially.

We certainly sit, but we rarely get anything of lasting value because the information is disconnected from our context and we are not engaged in collective learning because someone else decided for us what we needed to learn. In the end, the educators go back to their schools and classrooms, put the handouts on a shelf, and continue doing things the way they've always done them. The result: no collective learning, no development, no enhancement in practice, no advancement of a skillset. Not only are the educators not learning, but the indirect consequence is that they continue to teach students in ways that may not be effective.

Regardless of background, experience, interest, context, or ability, educators get lumped together for standardized professional development that addresses them more like cardboard cut-outs of teachers than complex human beings. They're merely widgets being shaped to take their places in the cogs of the factory model of education. There is no collaboration, no sharing of expertise and no development of a collective vision or goals.

THE HACK: COLLABORATE AND LEARN

At this point it is pretty clear to us that one-size-fits-all professional development is not a supportable option because we believe that individual passion projects and collective learning opportunities are the future of professional development in the world of education. Sessions where educators sit passively listening to one person deliver information may not be the best use of time. Sure, lecture-style presentations work sometimes, but not for extended periods of time, and not for every learner. We must shift to a collaborative process, we must provide options for learning, and we must encourage educators to take ownership of their own professional development.

All educators should have the power to personalize the professional development they participate in, even when it is collaborative and not individual in nature. Encourage them to be active learners who are comfortable sharing their expertise for the collective development of the organization. Give people time to learn together—with each other and from each other. For example, instead of having district or building administration plan and implement school-wide professional development, offer various options that will allow educators to take responsibility for their own personal and professional development.

If leaders would like their teachers to work collaboratively in a school or district setting, they might consider implementing an EdCamp model for professional learning. Teachers will learn from each other's expertise in such an environment, sending individuals' research and experiences far beyond their own classrooms to effect system-wide change. Recommending that teachers be allowed to choose their own preferred options means that school districts may need to redefine what counts as acceptable professional development so it is not limited to conferences, workshops, or graduate courses. Teachers will benefit from participating in a collegial book study, joining a Twitter chat, working with a PLC, developing a PLN on social media, experiencing an EdCamp, or even watching a webinar.

We can no longer look at personal development and professional development as two separate entities. Effective professional development must resonate on a personal level if it is going to be sustainable and serve as a catalyst for change in beliefs and practices. Tony's doctoral research into the impact of Twitter on principals' professional development found that the personal and professional are very much intertwined: Development often unfolds on a personal level as a result of social interactions before it can be enacted in a professional context. Based on the findings of this study, we would argue that when personal interest is piqued as a result of interactions with others, the level of investment increases and serves as a gateway for learning. Think about it for a second. If educators feel passionately about an idea and see value in it, the chances of their using it as a focal point for future learning—both individually and collectively—increases exponentially. Eventually, the idea will work its way into classroom practices.

Hacking traditional professional development experiences means giving people time to personalize their learning and then come together to learn, grow, and develop a collective vision and goals.

WHAT YOU CAN DO TOMORROW

- **Talk to teachers about what they need.** Set up a Google Calendar for the staff and have everyone sign up for three slots to check in with you about their passion project. Before school leaders begin planning for professional development opportunities, they must engage the staff in multiple conversations about needs, goals, and readiness levels. This should happen before, during and after the individual passion projects are completed because these conversations will help guide future collective learning opportunities.

- **Make collaborating about learning the norm.** Don't wait for formal professional development sessions to engage in learning. Instead, allow the learning to flow at all times. Share articles via email, post powerful infographics on bulletin boards, talk about data as a source of powerful information, and use every opportunity that the staff is physically together to engage in some type of collective learning that builds on individual expertise and passions.

- **Build common time into the schedule.** If we want collaboration among educators to be the norm, we must ensure that they have the time to make it happen. When constructing the master schedule for the school year, make sure teachers in the same grade level, team, or department have at least one common free period a week to talk, plan, and learn. If the school year has already started and the schedule is unchangeable, then arrange for coverage for one period every other week so the teachers can get together—get subs, cover the classes yourself, excuse a group of teachers from an event like a school-wide assembly, or see if minor changes can be made in the schedule for a specific date.

- **Create a Collective Learning chart to document learning.** Using a Google Doc, create a chart that tracks school-wide professional development. This Collective Learning chart features three columns: 1) **Existing knowledge:** areas teachers have already learned about and are implementing in their classrooms, 2) **Learning goals:** topics teachers would like to learn about, 3) **Understandings:** what teachers have learned as a result of their professional development. The Collective Learning chart serves several purposes. Teachers will be able to see where others in the school have expertise so they can develop communities of support. Recurring themes about what teachers want or need to learn emerge to guide PD. People can see who has similar needs or interests so they can get together and learn in any number of ways, such as discussing topics of interest, reading a common text, or processing student samples of work.

A BLUEPRINT FOR FULL IMPLEMENTATION

Step 1: Take a reading on staff readiness.

Making the shift from traditional professional development to a more progressive and self-directed model can be challenging because professional development is often rooted in tradition and culture. Any leaders who intend to redefine professional development should first make sure school culture is positive. For educators to be comfortable with a change of this nature, trust and respect must be at the core of the organization. The transition will be easier if you make choices available to ensure that all the educators have access to meaningful professional development regardless of their readiness levels. Some people may not be ready to shift too far away from traditional "sit and get" professional development, while others might be ready to mount an EdCamp.

Step 2: Rebrand staff meetings.

Although faculty meetings are part of any school culture, the time has come to jettison them if they generally only exist to share information. Most people dread meetings, especially after an already full day of work. If the information can be communicated via email or newsletter, there is no need to discuss it at a meeting. People's time is precious. Don't waste it by having them meet to listen to something they could quickly read on their own. If you're interested in how this might look, check out "Meet Me in the Cloud" in *Hacking Education* by Mark Barnes and Jennifer Gonzales.

Rebrand faculty meetings so it's clear that the occasion for staff to gather is professional development. At Cantiague we call staff gatherings "Faculty Enhancement Opportunities" (FEOs), and they are totally dedicated to professional development through collaborative learning opportunities. All logistical information gets shared in our weekly newsletter and so our time together is dedicated to learning, innovating, and enhancing our craft as a team. For example, the next time the staff gets together, have them break up into groups to pursue collective learning opportunities based on the needs of the students and organization.

Step 3: Make collective learning the norm.

The conversations about professional development need to happen in multiple ways: one-on-one, in small groups, and as an entire staff to ensure that everyone has some ownership of the learning process. The common thread here? All learning becomes collective in nature. After facilitating one-on-one check-ins with the staff, dedicate the rest of the faculty gatherings to learning opportunities that will happen in small groups and even some where the entire staff will work together. For example, when Cantiague began implementing the newest version of the Teachers College Units of Study for Reading and Writing Workshop, the entire process was collective in nature. We took the following steps:

- Teachers used common planning periods to begin exploring the units.

- One faculty enhancement opportunity each month was dedicated to district-wide grade-level meetings so teachers could share tips and ideas for successful implementation.

- Each grade-level team met with the principal once every six weeks for a literacy check-in where the principal served as the recorder and sounding board to help work out any kinks.

- When we came together as an entire staff, we dedicated several minutes to discussing the implementation in an effort to get a sense of how things were going in the K-5 spectrum.

Step 4: Start a collective learning committee.

Gather a team of teachers from every grade level or department and meet with them on a regular basis to discuss professional development needs. This think tank serves as the voice for the entire staff when determining what will work best for your school. Establish both short-term and long-term goals and share these plans with the staff so everyone knows what professional development to expect, when to expect it, and why it is happening.

Step 5: Initiate teacher-led sessions that support collective learning.

Educators will see the value in their own work if they can share ideas, resources, and plans with their colleagues. As leaders we cannot always assume we know what teachers need to learn and how they need to learn it, so we must give them the space to personalize their learning through initiatives such as passion projects. If you are not ready for personalized professional development, then at least try to facilitate differentiated topics so teachers can choose from several sessions that best meet their needs. As teachers build more capacity in this area of self-directed learning, you may even consider trying an EdCamp approach to professional and personal development.

OVERCOMING PUSHBACK

Unfortunately, not every educator in a school is open to learning. Reasons for negative attitudes to professional development could range from bad experiences with PD to believing that trained teachers have no need for further learning. Whatever the case, support of the entire staff is necessary to shift professional development practices, so ensure that every staff member has an entry point for learning. Be vigilant about not standardizing professional development opportunities so learning remains at the center of our work.

I have to tell my teachers what professional development sessions to attend because they don't take the initiative. One comment Tony has heard from many educators is that they don't have time to invest in their own learning because they are busy planning for the learning of their students. They feel stressed, overwhelmed, and too busy to carve out time to direct their own professional development, which often manifests in low building morale and no one taking initiative. These teachers don't want to have to think about professional learning, they don't want to plan for it, and they don't want to be actively engaged during it. They want handouts, links to resources, and a certificate showing they completed the session. As a result of such attitudes, some leaders feel compelled to tell teachers what session to attend and when to attend it because they perceive that some teachers have zero investment in their learning.

Helping educators shift from this fixed mindset to a hacker mindset requires some time and energy. Seek them out informally to discuss their practice, passions, and hopes for the students in their classes. Stress the importance of learning as an opportunity for growth and enhancement, and emphasize that they can direct it themselves, choosing topics of personal interest. We must help these individuals see the possibilities that self-directed learning will afford them person-ally. Just as engaged teachers model effective learning for their stu-dents, lead learners model it in their daily practices. Such obvious personal commitment to learning can be key to success with teachers as it becomes a new norm that is entrenched in school culture.

Teachers and school leaders who turn to social media sites such as Twitter can find other educators from around the globe who are looking to share, deliberate, and learn.

Our teachers would rather not be out of their classrooms for professional development and lose precious time with students. We have all heard pleas from teachers who don't want to attend a professional development session because they think it will be a waste of time that results in students missing learning. Unfortunately, these educators are generally speaking from expe-rience. They have probably sat through many one-size-fits-all professional development ses-sions that were not relevant to their work and thus led neither to changes in practice nor posi-tive impact on students. This is a reality that we must acknowledge and respect before we start changing things.

Teachers can be convinced that professional development is a good use of their time by making it worthwhile. We work diligently to ensure that our teachers have choices, entry points, and differentiated opportunities for professional development because we want it to be meaningful and sustainable. Fortunately, you can offer the uncertain teacher alternatives once you begin hacking the professional develop-ment in your school.

Teachers are going to think I am dumping my work on them. Many teachers are accustomed to having building and district administra-tors take care of planning and implementing professional develop-ment. Whether someone is brought into the school to lead learning or teachers are sent out to a workshop, teachers have become used to and comfortable with someone else planning the learning for them. These teachers could potentially feel like the work of the administrator is being dumped on them once the topic of teacher-led professional development and self-directed learning comes up. Take it slowly and help them understand that they are being empowered to personalize their learning on their own terms; they are not necessarily doing someone else's work, they are just taking control of their own.

The teacher-led professional development committee can be instrumental in helping others to understand why this hack is necessary and how they can successfully navigate the changes. When teachers talk to each other, support each other, and encourage each other, experiences tend to progress in much more positive ways and the impact leads to long-lasting transformations. Arrange for staff to meet in small groups that can be facilitated by members of the professional development committee. These small group meetings will provide the concerned teachers a space to air out their issues so that they feel heard and validated. The committee members can work with their colleagues to understand that this shift in professional development is a powerful opportunity.

THE HACK IN ACTION

Based on our experiences as connected educators, one of the first hacks we suggest you make to professional development is to expose staff to the power of being connected online. More and more educators are turning to social media to accelerate their learning and enhance their development. Be aware that forcing teachers to incorporate the use of platforms such as Twitter and Voxer into their professional development plans may be counterproductive. Rather than alienating those who may initially feel apprehensive, it's better to introduce the possibilities and let individuals decide for themselves how connected they want to be. Many educators maintain that they made the decision to get connected using a tool like Twitter mainly to alleviate feelings of isolation and were delighted to find that they gained access to a dynamic platform that accelerated their learning in ways they did not anticipate.

Teachers and school leaders who turn to social media sites such as Twitter can find other educators from around the globe who are looking to share, deliberate, and learn. Eventually, repeated interactions online may transform into a Personal Learning Network (PLN), whereby educators connect in a linked system of relationships. Participants are effusive about the impact of the PLN—people are willing to share, collaborate, and trust each other because using social learning networks encourages a level of transparency and openness between members. The structure of the PLN and the dynamic nature of how information is shared on Twitter are common features of virtual communities of practice because of the low barriers—easy access to people and ideas regardless of traditional barriers such as geographical location—and active, self-directed nature of the learning.

We believe it is clear that both digital and "real time" learning experiences benefit from having features of communities of practice and participatory cultures embedded in them. Whether the communities of practice start as a grade-level team or include thousands of educators in a PLN, we need to encourage educators to learn from each other. We know that the relationships at the core of the PLN are dynamic and fluid, and the resulting interactions serve as the foundation for powerful learning. Teachers and school leaders who avail themselves of these experiences have realized profound impact on both their personal and professional development. All educators need access to this type of learning, which would allow them to share their expertise but also to lean on an expert when learning about something new.

Tony's Story

Becoming a connected educator has sparked powerful personal and professional transformations for me. My PLN consists of thousands of educators who share resources, blog posts, and perspectives. My connection to this virtual community has been the catalyst for significant professional development, shaping personal beliefs and opinions about education, and also equipping me with practical tools that I can immediately put into practice in my school community. For example, after an active discussion about teacher observations with my PLN I started using Evernote and Google Docs instead of Word documents to write up my observations. This shift to cloud-based tools afforded me more flexibility because I was able to complete an observation from any computer and easily offer teachers a link to the document to collaborate on the final version.

Another example of a PLN-inspired change that is more school-wide in nature came as a result of participating in a few sessions of the weekly #PTChat. This Twitter chat discusses parent/teacher and home/school relationships every Wednesday night. After engaging in several weekly chats and thinking about how the community perceived our school, I was inspired to use Twitter to tell our school story. When I began to "flatten the walls" of our school by sharing pictures and descriptions of school moments a few years ago, I was the only person in our school tweeting pictures and captions, but by the start of the current school year every classroom had its own Twitter account and teachers were actively using the platform to tell the stories of their classrooms. Community response to this practice has been overwhelmingly positive, with most commenters referring to an appreciation for our high levels of transparency and the sense of trust and pride that have been nurtured as a result.

Teachers need learning that is personalized, relevant, and easily applied to their context. Providing professional development with these qualities will encourage educators to be actively engaged in self-directed learning experiences. As a result, they will access information, ideas, and resources that will enhance their craft and have a positive impact on their schools. Rather than waiting for someone else to decide on and implement professional development, educators can actively look to address personal and professional goals once they have the tools to do so. Instead of simply being receivers of professional development, educators can be generators of information and catalysts of others' professional development, both within and beyond their school settings.

Whether using a social media platform to discuss educational issues with a PLN, discussing teaching strategies in a grade-level group, developing a common language of learning in a subject area, or facilitating a session during an EdCamp, reimagining professional development makes it relevant and effective. When we give educators ownership and control of their learning, professional development will resonate on a personal level, which is critical to its sustainability and overall impact.

CHANGE THE MINDSET
Eradicate deficit thinking

I do not fix problems. I fix my thinking.
Then problems fix themselves.
—LOUISE HAY, AUTHOR AND MOTIVATIONAL SPEAKER

THE PROBLEM: EDUCATORS DEFER TO DEFICIT THINKING

THE MORE WE interact with educators from around the country, the more we understand how pervasively the deficit mindset saturates the world of education. Between the two of us, we have been working in the field of education for almost forty years and we cannot tell you how many times we have heard statements that start with, "These kids can't learn this because…" or, "Those teachers can't implement that instructional model because…" or, "This community of families can't do that because…." As soon as a sentence begins that way, we know the end will be negative. Generally, the speaker will refer to socioeconomic status; geographical context and perceptions of a certain neighborhood or community; or some other perceived disadvantage affecting students, educators, or the community at large. These speakers manifest their deficit mindset in their words. The impact of speaking and acting from such a point of view can be devastating to students, families, and entire school communities.

The deficit model of education has been around since the one-room schoolhouse. Although we have come to associate it with labeling special education students or students living in impoverished communities, its impact doesn't end with children. When we identify a child, a teacher, or a school with what it lacks—usually one fixed and negative attribute—we limit an exceedingly complex system to that determiner. No possibility, no potential exists for it in the mind of the beholder without recourse to that label, both as a defining mark and as an obstacle. The more pervasive this negative mindset the more the label determines possibilities for children, teachers, schools, and practices within a school community.

The time has come to hack leadership by embracing an innovator's mindset, an opportunity mindset, a growth mindset, a positive mindset, or whatever you choose to call the opposite of a deficit mindset.

For example, we know of numerous school leaders who are hesitant to implement a Bring Your Own Device (BYOD) model of technology because they fear the unknown multitude of things that could go wrong. This focus on the problem clearly limits their ability to integrate technology into the school. It's especially problematic when you consider the attitude they communicate: The majority of children in those schools are untrustworthy or untrainable. This deficit thinking can stifle a community because collective fear reframes opportunities into roadblocks or barriers.

Sadly, the deficit mindset is pervasive and its impact far-reaching. It's evident in the school leaders who don't want to use the reading or writing workshop model in their literacy block because their teachers "aren't ready" for it and instead buy a scripted program that delineates what should be happening every minute of the day. It's there in the classroom where children aren't encouraged to access challenging materials or concepts because they "can't handle" it. Educators can have a negative impact when they direct more attention to problems and pitfalls than possibilities and opportunities.

THE HACK: ERADICATE DEFICIT THINKING

Tony's Story

The deficit thinking model was something I struggled with as a parent when I was considering how to tell my son that I was gay. In the months leading up to that day, many people bombarded me with negative opinions: "Your son can't handle the gay thing." "Your son can't understand the gay thing." "Your son isn't ready for the gay thing." In spite of these naysayers, I felt like my son was ready, so I put aside the drawbacks and deficiencies that other people had suggested and chose not to participate in that mindset. On *the* day, I woke up with one idea: I think my son can handle this.

Our exchange ended with his giving me a hug and reassuring me that he would love me no matter who I loved. I bit my tongue hard to hold back the tears because Paul's accepting response showed such maturity, composure, compassion, and love. I had been right: He could handle the gay thing. Even in that incredibly difficult moment, he was able to access the opposite of a deficit mindset—he was open, positive, and willing to look at things from a new perspective. Instead of limiting ourselves, we moved beyond potential obstacles into a relationship characterized by overabundance rather than deficiencies.

I share this personal reflection as a model for the kind of surplus of joy and learning we can generate in our schools when we eliminate deficit thinking. It is time to move away from a focus on deficiencies to give our children the space to learn, grow, fail, try again, and succeed on their terms. They need our support and encouragement, not our preconceived notions of the disadvantages that limit them. With minds full of possibilities, we build confidence by considering all the things our children *can* do, not all the things we think they *can't* do. Focus on children's strengths and build those up instead of harping on their weaknesses and trying to fix them.

Let's let go of our fears of failure, our negative perceptions of teacher effectiveness, and empower our teachers to make the best decisions possible for their students instead of insisting they follow scripted curriculum or zero-tolerance policies. Let's support and encourage their work in the classroom by engaging families in meaningful ways as we become true partnership schools. It's time to stop blaming families for all the problems that afflict a community and work together.

The time has come to hack leadership by embracing an innovator's mindset, an opportunity mindset, a growth mindset, a positive mindset, or whatever you choose to call the opposite of a deficit mindset. Our children, educators, school communities, and families deserve the opportunity to experience success by building on their strengths.

WHAT YOU CAN DO TOMORROW

Making the shift from a deficit mindset to a more positive one should not be incredibly difficult because the truth is that we want to see our students succeed and thrive. Unfortunately, even with that reality we still tend to focus on the negative and see our neediest children as being broken somehow. Instead of trying to fix the child, let's repair the way we think about students and figure out how we can best support and encourage them.

- **Find out what parents want for their children.** The best way to avoid slipping into a focus on deficiencies is to find out about possibilities. Talk to parents and find out what they hope and dream for their children. We need to explore their goals and figure out ways to make that potential a reality. Make sure every family has an entry point for engagement regardless of language, culture, socioeconomic status, or time constraints. Focus on face-to-face exchanges—nothing tops shaking hands and exchanging a smile as an opening for a congenial relationship. If families can't meet you in person, send a note home or contact them using email, social media, or even video chatting. There are dozens of ways to connect with families who can't get to the school, so let's stop using that as an excuse. Be sure to offer translations whenever possible for non-English speakers. They deserve to get information in a way they can understand. Family engagement should be neither a burden nor a challenge; use it as an opportunity to learn more about our students and to battle the deficit mindset.

- **Talk to the children.** Start facilitating relationships by scheduling times to gather with specific children—have lunch with a group of kids, facilitate a book club during recess, or start a before- or after-school club for kids to just drop by, play games, talk, and connect. Personal conversations can happen informally in the hallway, lunchroom, or playground, but begin with more intentional interactions. Choose the option that feels most comfortable for you, but build time into your schedule to establish healthy relationships with trust and respect. Connecting with students on a personal level can be critical to their academic success. Children feel like they can accomplish anything when educators show sincere interest. They thrive when educators believe in them and support them.

- **Seek to understand what children can do.** Start noticing what children are capable of instead of concentrating on their deficits. More often than not, the inclination is to focus on the negative. When this happens, shift your thinking to reframe the problem and see it as an opportunity. An educator's primary responsibility is to access the talents and gifts in every child to maximize his or her school experience. Jay Posick, who is a middle school principal in Wisconsin, works directly in the classroom to learn about his students' strengths. He sets up a calendar so teachers can book a time for him to come into their classrooms and lead or support instruction. He might teach a lesson, facilitate a small group, or support a specific student based on the teacher's request. As a result, Jay has come to know his students as learners and thus appreciates their strengths and readiness levels.

- **Use data to identify strengths.** Instead of using data just to target needs, take a second look at it to see how you might target strengths. Data that pinpoints strengths helps educators teach to students' areas of expertise and empowers students to feel successful. This focus on strengths allows us to celebrate student success, but also to use their strengths as a foundation for improving skills and to address areas where skills are good but have room for growth. You can begin seeking out strengths as soon as a new student registers at your school by administering a standardized test such as the MIDAS (Multiple Intelligences Developmental Assessment Scales), created by Branton Shearer. This test measures students' multiple intelligences. Use the results to create a student profile that can help inform the teachers' instructional decisions.

A BLUEPRINT FOR FULL IMPLEMENTATION

Step 1: Build capacity.

Most teachers have been trained to recognize deficiencies in student work as the central act in assessment. Traditionally, educators have focused on fixing what students are getting wrong instead of acknowledging what they are doing well. As a result, the shift to a different mindset may feel forced at first. One way to counter habitual focus on deficits would be to begin systematically placing attention on strengths. For example, asking educators to notice two strengths for every weakness exhibited by a student is a small start, but a start nonetheless. Focus on actions and process rather than qualities such as intelligence or comments such as "good job" to reinforce the students' sense of agency rather than traits over which they have no control. Our goal is to provide feedback that facilitates the learning for students and doesn't bring it to a screeching halt by focusing only on weaknesses.

Step 2: Model, model, model.

You can model mindset as a leader by ensuring that you validate the strong work of both teachers and students. Your voice and actions hold weight with both these segments of the learning community: What you value will set the tone for what others value as well. Ensure that your comments are specific and sincere, and that you validate excellent, not merely adequate, work so that those around you find aspirational goals. Where work is not consistently excellent, indicate specific bits that are working well so they continue being implemented and become the norm. If the entire team works consistently to build capacity and recognize strengths while not ignoring areas of need, the common mindset will gradually shift to become a supportive one that seeks and produces excellence.

Step 3: Encourage educators to learn something difficult.

Having teachers reverse roles by focusing on their own learning ensures that they experience the discomfort of acquiring new and challenging ideas. Developing empathy for the children's daily experiences will encourage teachers to find ways to help students progress without harping on their weaknesses. Like our students, we prefer to have our strengths rather than our deficits reinforced as we learn; indeed, most adults feel embarrassed and discouraged when they find their weaknesses get attention. For many educators, it has been a long time since they struggled or felt incompetent in a learning environment, and this reminder will spark recognition of how many students feel in school.

Continually expanding knowledge with new experiences ideally extends to developing a broader perspective, a critical factor in altering mindset.

For example, at Cantiague we have children facilitate professional development sessions for teachers during our faculty meetings. The children choose an area of expertise, typically involving technology, and develop a "lesson plan" to teach someone to use that resource. After trying their lesson out on a group of classmates, the children are invited to a faculty meeting to teach the staff. We have had children of all ages present at staff meetings, and their presentations have been outstanding learning experiences for both parties. Lessons generally begin with an introduction of the tool, a quick example of how to use the tool, and support for small groups of teachers as they try out the tool. The students become lead learners as they help their teachers enhance their skillset; the teachers remember what it is like to sit on the other side of the desk and witness students demonstrating their strengths.

Step 4: Give kids access to diverse learning opportunities.

Expand beyond math and literacy so that all students can develop their abilities. In this time of high-stakes testing and standards-based instruction, horror stories frequently circulate about schools that teach only math and literacy because those are the only areas being tested. In this kind of environment, some students never get to provide evidence of their strengths; others cannot develop potential talents. If we want all of our students to be successful, we need to give them access to diverse learning opportunities across all content areas. Children need to experience the arts and physical fitness, and to develop social/emotional skills. We want to nurture a positive mindset in our students by introducing them to a broad range of learning, leading them to discover aptitudes and abilities across many subjects.

Step 5: Celebrate the awesome things happening in your school.

Continue to broaden the focus from individual to community as you highlight strengths. Move beyond individual work as you celebrate the strengths of your community as a whole. Todd Whitaker recommends creating a weekly staff newsletter so the teachers can see what colleagues are doing. Such a publication will spotlight all the amazing work of individuals and underscore the vigorous growth in your school. First, decide on the best format for the newsletter—it can be paper, email, Google Doc or blog (Cantiague uses Blogger). Then, decide on the format of the newsletter by listing the things you want to include.

The Cantiague newsletter includes a "Curriculum Connection" section, which is just a general reflection on how things are going in the building; an "#EduWins" section where Tony spotlights three amazing things he saw happen in specific classrooms; a section where Tony shares three or four current blog posts from Twitter that are worth reading, ensuring that the newsletter addresses learning and not just information sharing; a calendar of the upcoming week at Cantiague; and some general reminders about upcoming events.

This year the newsletter incorporated a "Staff Blogs" section where different staff members (and sometimes students) share a professional or personal reflection. Yes, the newsletter allows the administration to disseminate information that people can read on their own so they don't need to sit through an informational meeting, but it also serves as a form of professional development, becoming the impetus for trying and sharing new ideas. Although the "#EduWins" section used to be the only space where amazing work was spotlighted, the "Staff Blogs" section also allows educators to share their own awesomeness, knowledge, and experiences. However, it might be wise to hold off on including such a section in a brand new newsletter, since there has to be a level of trust for people to share in a vulnerable way. The effectiveness of the newsletter, and particularly the staff blog posts, is evident in increased activity on the blog's comment section; more conversations in the hallways; and free flow of ideas between grade levels, specialists, and support staff.

OVERCOMING PUSHBACK

Regardless of context or setting, every educator periodically falls victim to the deficit mindset. Sometimes the tendency to focus on the negative or treat children as problems to be fixed feels overwhelming. For the elementary teacher obsessing about that one child who hasn't moved up on the reading level scale or the school leader worrying about a small group of teachers who resist curricular initiatives, the negative outweighs the positive. Concentrating on what's wrong stifles any ability to move forward productively. Fortunately, a detour into deficit thinking doesn't have to be permanent—with some basic reframing, problems can transform into opportunities.

But "these children" can't handle this stuff. This comment exemplifies the dangers of the deficit mindset. When Knapp and Shields

(1990) wrote about the deficit model in schools, they noted that educators set lower standards for certain students because their behavior, language use, or values did not match those that were expected in school, and related instances of teachers referring to the students as "these children," a phrase which oozes with negativity and anticipated failure. We've all heard some educator complain about the inability of "these children" to handle rigorous curriculum because of their perceived limitations.

More often than not, "these children" refers to students who live in an impoverished community, belong to a visible minority, or have been labeled "special education" because of learning deficits. They may not be considered smart enough or engaged enough to learn, or they lack the schema to make sense of the content. Whatever the reason, some educators are so convinced that the children won't be able to handle challenging content that they never expose them to it. Thus the self-fulfilling prophecy: Students will perform exactly how we think they are capable of performing. Our expectations can transform a child's life, so why keep them low? If we set the bar high, we will be pleasantly surprised to see how many of our students can soar over it. We must begin by noting their strengths. Children are often much more capable than adults give them credit for. We believe that if educators frame learning experiences as opportunities to succeed, most students will rise to the challenge regardless of readiness levels.

Hacking the deficit mindset can best be accomplished by framing every problem as an opportunity to learn from a new experience.

Our families won't get involved: It's not that type of community. Most families want to be as involved as possible in their children's education, but we're cautious about conflating individual families with the community at large. We cannot make sweeping generalizations about a community based on our perceptions or opinions—that is the deficit mindset at work. You may have to adjust your expectations to allow parental involvement to take the form parents are capable of offering. For example, parents who are immigrants or who don't speak English may not be able to help their children with a homework assignment, but that doesn't mean they don't care or that they can't make sure it gets done. The parents who work multiple jobs just to afford the rent may not be able to attend a parent/teacher conference. We must start by assuming that every family wants to be involved and that our job should be to figure out ways to involve them.

An easy place to start is with face-to-face interactions. Host a breakfast at the start of the school year and open it up to all families. If you would like it to be a bit more structured, go to Doodle.com, set up a schedule of your available times, and email the link out to groups of families, possibly ten at a time, so they can schedule specific appointments with you to meet one-on-one. Finally, if that all seems like too much because of the size of your community, create a Google Survey and get it out to all families—email the link, paste the link on your website, or even print out QR codes and send it home with kids. The onus for getting families involved in the educational experience lies with the school leader. We must model that we will do whatever we must do to engage a family.

Our school does not have the resources to compete with that other school. Many schools have limited funds and scarce resources. Typically, that becomes the excuse for not trying something new and any possible innovation ends there. "We don't have X so we can't do Y." Look for possibilities and not obstacles. Plenty of exciting endeavors require little or no money. Want to have access to more technology but have no money to buy hardware? Implement a BYOD policy and let the kids bring in their own devices. Chances are, the majority of your students will bring one in, as smartphone access cuts across socioeconomic boundaries.

Encourage children to share their devices with those who have none, because sharing a device is better than not engaging with one at all. Want to redesign your learning space so it is comfortable for the children to learn but don't have the money to buy new furniture? Try asking friends, family, and students if they have gently-used furniture to donate to the classroom. Even one couch can change the feel of your room. Want a new classroom library but have no money to buy books? Start a DonorsChoose page to raise the funding. Chances are, many people will donate. Students in less affluent schools deserve the same quality of education as any other students. We must get creative to ensure that our students have every opportunity possible.

THE HACK IN ACTION

One of the first places to change the mindset is day-to-day instruction. In many schools, teachers are still doing the majority of the talking and teaching because they are not confident in relinquishing control to the students. Children do need some direct instruction, but beyond that they need to be experiencing things on their own. Begin hacking the deficit mindset by shifting instruction so children are doing more and teachers are doing less.

We recently heard from an elementary teacher who works in the New York City public school system with a population of students of predominantly low socioeconomic status, either immigrants or first-generation Americans. Early on in the year the principal and other teachers told this teacher to keep it simple and not expect much because, although the children were well-behaved, they couldn't handle much content. By the end of the school year, this teacher had the children reading and analyzing Shakespeare, writing their own historical fiction picture books, and facilitating their own book clubs.

His students were no different from the children in the next classroom, but the other kids spent the whole day sitting at their desks flipping from one workbook to another and engaging in lessons dominated by the teacher. Every child was expected to learn the same content, in the same way, during the same timeframe, and none of them was being pushed to think critically. In contrast, the teacher we met empowered his students to pursue challenging learning experiences, telling them not to worry about failing because he was there to help them up and support them. He facilitated healthy relationships and set high standards. And guess what? His kids loved zooming past conventional expectations.

Hacking the deficit mindset can best be accomplished by framing every problem as an opportunity to learn from a new experience. Yes, the world of education is filled with many barriers, but as school leaders we determine what impact those barriers have on our communities. We can allow them to stay in place for teachers and students to stumble over or detour around, and thereby limit learning, or we can do our best to remove them, giving access to new possibilities where they can thrive and prosper.

We won't be able to overcome the deficit model if we don't invest our hearts and souls into the work we do each day. We need to start by sharing our humanity—our passions, interests, and fears—with our students because this is how we build relationships. Also, we need to have as much fun as possible. Don't save the "fun time" for free time on Friday; instead, give the kids a chance to have fun during math, reading, and social studies every day because when kids are having fun the tone in the classroom changes for the better.

A fun classroom where children feel safe and excited about daily opportunities can easily become a hotbed for innovation, one in which kids get used to failing and trying again, because focus is on all that the kids can do instead of on what they can't do.

CONCLUSION
Be like water

WATER IS TRULY an amazing element. It literally shapes the land around it with constant movement and subtle pressure. It always finds a way, thanks to its gentle persistence.

The tools in this text can help you be a leader whose abilities are like water. Find the smallest opening that you didn't even realize existed and create a channel for staff members, students, and families to pass through on their way to greatness. Help form the environment around you by engaging in relationships with your team and empowering them to grow their own leadership capacity. Nourish those around you by fostering mutual trust and respect so all members of the school community own the process of learning and leading. Amplify and accelerate your message by accessing various social media platforms and leveraging the talents of those around you who want to see great things happen for kids. Remember, it is always about doing what is best for kids even when it's not comfortable or easy.

We also know that too much water at one time can be destructive, just as too many initiatives can overwhelm your organization. Too much can be as detrimental as too little because it makes everyone feel unsettled and unbalanced. Like water, excess can drown everyone in its path.

The truth is, people try to do the best work they can and often aim for awesome. Not too many people wake up in the morning and say that they can't wait to be average today. Average is not a goal you set out to reach, it is a place where you end up for any number of reasons and much like a ship that runs aground in shallow water, educators can get stuck at average. Educators can experience a drought where the possibilities seem limited and the future is dim. As leaders who embrace a hacker mentality, we can change that by offering support, encouragement, and opportunities. If you are consistently looking to hack leadership, you are always seeking greatness in yourself and those around you, from the teachers to the families to the students and the bus drivers. Foster everyone's success, because they are working toward kids' best interests.

When we reach that goal where the water has perfectly permeated the space for optimal growth and nourishment, we create schools that students, staff, and parents love; we create schools that avoid the deficit mentality and embrace the opportunity to innovate and make learning; we create schools where the staff are superstars and our hiring practices ensure that we will only get better; we create schools that empower everyone to promote a common vision as a result of distributive leadership; we create schools that put kids at the center and focus on building a healthy C.U.L.T.U.R.E. Hacking leadership refocuses the trajectory of the water.

OTHER BOOKS IN THE HACK LEARNING SERIES

HACKING EDUCATION
10 Quick Fixes For Every School

By Mark Barnes (@markbarnes19) & Jennifer Gonzalez (@cultofpedagogy)

In the bestselling *Hacking Education*, Mark Barnes and Jennifer Gonzalez employ decades of teaching experience and hundreds of discussions with education thought leaders, to show you how to find and hone the quick fixes that every school and classroom need. Using a Hacker's mentality, they provide one Aha moment after another with 10 Quick Fixes For Every School—solutions to everyday problems and teaching methods that any teacher or administrator can implement immediately.

"Barnes and Gonzalez don't just solve problems; they turn teachers into hackers—a transformation that is right on time."
— Don Wettrick, author of *Pure Genius*

MAKE WRITING
5 Teaching Strategies That Turn Writers Workshop Into a Maker Space

By Angela Stockman (@angelastockman)

Everyone's favorite education blogger and writing coach, Angela Stockman, turns teaching strategies and practice upside down in the bestselling, *Make Writing*. She spills you out of your chair, shreds your lined paper, and launches you and your writer's workshop into the maker space! Stockman provides five right-now writing strategies that reinvent instruction and inspire both young and adult writers to express ideas with tools and in ways that have rarely, if ever, been considered. Make Writing is a fast-paced journey inside Stockman's Western New York Young Writer's Studio, alongside the students there who learn how to write and how to make, employing Stockman's unique teaching methods.

HACKING ASSESSMENT
10 Ways to Go Gradeless in a Traditional Grades School

By Starr Sackstein (@mssackstein)

In the bestselling *Hacking Assessment*, award-winning teacher and world-renowned formative assessment expert Starr Sackstein unravels one of education's oldest mysteries: How to assess learning without grades— even in a school that uses numbers, letters, GPAs, and report cards. While many educators can only muse about the possibility of a world without grades, teachers like Sackstein are reimagining education. In this unique, eagerly-anticipated book, Sackstein shows you exactly how to create a remarkable no-grades classroom like hers, a vibrant place where students grow, share, thrive, and become independent learners who never ask, "What's this worth?"

HACKING THE COMMON CORE
10 Strategies for Amazing Learning in a Standardized World

By Michael Fisher (@fisher1000)

In *Hacking the Common Core,* longtime teacher and CCSS specialist Mike Fisher shows you how to bring fun back to learning, with 10 amazing hacks for teaching the Core in all subjects, while engaging students and making learning fun. Fisher's experience and insights help teachers and parents better understand close reading, balancing fiction and nonfiction, using projects with the Core and much more. *Hacking the Common Core* provides read-tonight-implement-tomorrow strategies for teaching the standards in fun and engaging ways, improving teaching and learning for students, parents, and educators.

ABOUT THE AUTHORS

Dr. Tony Sinanis, who is a proud dad to Paul, is currently a Lead Learner at Cantiague Elementary School in Jericho, New York. Cantiague was named a 2012 National Blue Ribbon School. Tony received the national 2013 Bammy Award for Elementary School Principal of the Year and the 2014 New York State Elementary Principal of the Year Award. As part of his doctoral studies at the University of Pennsylvania, Tony studied the relationship between active participation on Twitter and the professional development of principals. Tony is active on Twitter (@TonySinanis) and serves as the founder and co-moderator of #NYedchat. Tony is also the co-host of the Successful Schools podcast with Dr. Joe Sanfelippo. Finally, Tony has co-authored two books for Corwin Press with Joe: *The Power of Branding: Telling Your School's Story* and *Principal Professional Development: Leading Learning in the Digital Age.*

Dr. Joe Sanfelippo is the Superintendent of the Fall Creek School District in Fall Creek, Wisconsin. Joe holds a BA in Elementary and Early Childhood Education from St. Norbert College, an MS in Educational Psychology from the University of Wisconsin-Milwaukee, an MS in Educational Leadership, and a PhD in Leadership, Learning, and Service from Cardinal Stritch University. Joe is also an adjunct professor in the Educational Leadership Department at Viterbo University. Joe has taught Kindergarten, 2nd Grade, and 5th Grade. He was also a school counselor and coach prior to taking on an elementary principalship in 2005. He has been the Superintendent in Fall Creek since 2011. Joe co-hosts the Successful Schools Podcast, and co-authored *The Power of Branding-Telling Your School's Story* and *Principal Professional Development: Leading Learning in a Digital Age.* He was selected as one of 117 Future Ready Superintendents in 2014 by the US Department of Education and attended a summit at the White House. Joe has been a featured speaker in multiple states in the areas of Advancing the Use of Social Media in School Districts, Creating a Culture of Yes, Professional Growth for Staff, and Organizational and Systems Change. Go Crickets!

PUBLICATIONS

Times 10 is helping all education stakeholders improve every aspect of teaching and learning. We are committed to solving big problems with simple ideas. We bring you content from experts, shared through multiple channels, including books, podcasts, and an array of social networks. Our mantra is simple: Read it today; fix it tomorrow. Stay in touch with us at HackLearning.org, at #HackLearning on Twitter, and on the Hack Learning Facebook page.